THE LEADERSHIP
INTEGRITY
CHALLENGE

THE LEADERSHIP INTEGRITY CHALLENGE

HOW TO ASSESS AND FACILITATE EMOTIONAL MATURITY

Edward E. Morler, M.B.A., Ph.D.

Sanai Publishing
Sonoma, California

Sanai Publishing
1140 Brockman Dr.
Sonoma, CA 95476
(707) 935-7798; Fax, (707) 935-3642
www.sanaipublishing.com

Printed in the United States of America

LCCN: 2005929121
ISBN: 0-9768643-0-4

With love and affection, I dedicate this book to my wife, De Morler. Her love, patience and support have helped me look into my own self-imposed limitations and inspired me to greater sensitivity and compassion. Because of her, I continue to be more of who I am becoming.

ACKNOWLEDGMENTS

The contents of *The Leadership Integrity Challenge* is a synthesis of concepts and practical applications from many disciplines: philosophy, psychology, organizational theory, quantum mechanics, chaos theory, metaphysics, religion, education and business. The basic concepts and dynamics are not new. They have been expounded as ideals since the dawn of civilization. The only thing original here is how they are organized and presented.

Many individuals have contributed to this current integration. Their critiques and suggestions have been invaluable and are very much appreciated. Any mistakes, omissions, awkwardness or lack of clarity are solely my responsibility.

I want first to thank my wife De for her loving patience and support for a project that became much more time consuming than anticipated. Secondly, I am indebted to General "Jack" Chain, who patiently read a number of drafts, made many valuable suggestions and became a good friend in the process. Similarly, Lou Thompson, C.E.O. of the National Investor Relations Institute and Jack Krol, former C.E.O. of DuPont also devoted significant time reviewing and providing insightful comments on focus and direction. Many thanks to developmental editor, Mary Lobig-Giles and copy editors Katrina Mather, Kelly Crawley, and Ricky Weisbroth. In addition, I would like to express my appreciation to Lorien Fenton and Debra van Stigt for all their helpful and professional administrative support. I wish to express special thanks to Amelia Behm, my exceptionally competent associate of seventeen years who tolerated, with aplomb, the numerous attempts of earlier versions.

Many others have reviewed various sections or drafts and provided feedback and support. These include: James Andracchi, Acquisitions Integration Manager, Metavante; Huguette Anhalt, screenwriter; David Arrigo, Senior Chief Petty Officer, U.S.N.; Eleanor Bloxham, President, The Value Alliance and author of *Value-Led Organizations*; Melissa Booth, Executive Director, Executive Leadership Institute; Robert Booth, E.V.P. and Senior Credit Officer, Enterprise Bank; Jack Carlsen, Senior Chief Petty Officer, U.S.N.; Betty and Richard Connor, lifelong friends; Judy and Bill Elbring, Cofounders, LifePartners; Rich Everett, C.O.O., West Marine; Bruce Fabric, M.D., Psychiatrist; Dawson Faulk, entrepreneur; Ben Gerson, Senior Editor, *Harvard Business Review*; Andrew Hahn, Psy. D., Founder, *Guided Self Healing*; Lois Hart, Ed. D., Executive Director, The Woman's Leadership Institute; Ellen Heffes, Managing Editor, *Financial Executives International*; John Horen-Kates, President, Vail Leadership Institute; Carla Jacobs, C.E.O., Jacobs Creative; Bill Keener, Regional Credit Director, Regions Bank; Jack Labanauskas, Editor, *Enneagram Monthly*; Fleur Lee, artist; Latoya Love, student, University of Wisconsin; Richard Love, philosopher; Ellen Masterson, Partner, PricewaterhouseCoopers; Ron Morgan, Director of H.R., Nektar Therapeutics; Ron Ostertag, former C.E.O., General Semiconductor, Inc.; Rod Pieper, Executive Coach; James Sprayregen, Head, Worldwide Restructuring Group, Kirkland and Ellis; John Santi, Managing Director, Stanford Group Co.; Robert Vanourek, Chairman, Vail Leadership Institute; Orlando Villanueva-Cortez, Professor (retired), Purdue University; Lesley Ward, Ph.D., Psychologist; Larry West, E.V.P. (retired), Banc One; Marjorie Winegrow, Director, SAGE Scholars Program, UC Berkeley.

Thank you all.

CONTENTS

FOREWORD

by General John T. "Jack" Chain, U.S.A.F., Retired
Former Commander-in-Chief of the Strategic Air Command

The Leadership Integrity Challenge is a seminal work on a critically important subject. It deserves the attention of everyone who desires a world where integrity is not a cliché, but a living presence. I have been very fortunate in my life and career to have known and worked with people and organizations of integrity. Regardless of the pressures, which can be many, and the consequences of decisions, which can be significant, living in an integral environment creates clarity and an inner sense of what is right action. When that is missing, chaos abounds and bad things happen, including losing a sense of the meaning and value of integrity itself. For sanity and good judgment to prevail, an environment of integrity is not simply desirable—it is necessary. Integrity truly is the vital factor.

Recent corporate scandals have demonstrated a level of greed and fraud, the likes of which we have not seen before. Nevertheless, they have also been a gift, for they have created an awareness of the vital importance of integrity and the huge cost of its lack. These scandals have been a powerful stimulus to look more deeply at this problem. Issues of governance, of compliance, of potential conflicts of interest, of reporting and accounting procedures are being looked at with more scrutiny than ever before. Some of what comes out of this will be helpful. Some may only divert us from the underlying issue of how we are to create an integral environment, not simply ensure compliance to some arbitrary set of rules and laws. Clear standards and better procedures are necessary but while they may be contributing factors, they are not in themselves causative or transformative.

Dealing with causative and transformative factors is what *The Leadership Integrity Challenge* addresses in-depth. In it, Dr. Morler has taken this much-talked-about but little understood subject and not only made it understandable, but also provided a model and means to expand its presence. He looks at integrity from its many facets—how it relates to our maturity and sense of purpose; how it affects our ability to deal with change; how it influences our perceptions, attitudes, authenticity, contributions, and leadership potential as well as our ability to enjoy life.

Dr. Morler clarifies how you and I tick the way we do, how we can let go of our self-imposed limitations and facilitate others to do the same, and how we can choose to live an empowered life with integrity at its core and do so with others of like intention. He expands on and beyond emotional intelligence to emotional maturity and shows how its development is key to creating more integrity in our lives.

The Leadership Integrity Challenge has application for all walks of life, across all cultures, from personal growth to leadership development. It has a breadth and depth that deserves careful study. Anyone who sits back and puts their feet up will find many useful applications. It is particularly useful for leaders who are serious about developing an integral organization. It should be a priority read for any executive, supervisor, manager, or aspiring leader. I hope it gets the attention it deserves.

Jack Chain
May 2005

INTRODUCTION

Live your best and act your best and think your best today, for today is the sure preparation for tomorrow and all other tomorrows that follow.

—Harriet Martineau

When Bruce was mistakenly given a one hundred-dollar bill instead of the ten dollars due him, he hesitated for a moment, then mumbled "thank you" and quickly walked away.

Carol didn't say anything when she noticed her boss padding expenses. After all, her review was coming up and, besides, it wasn't her money.

Peter knew there was a potential conflict of interest, but the "smart people" were doing it and had been for years. Not going along seemed not only naive but foolish.

We do not have to look far to find numerous examples of self-serving or dishonest behavior. We live in a world that largely views integrity as inconvenient, impractical, or naive. The magnitude and crassness of recent corporate scandals have awakened public awareness to the extent and cost of such irresponsible behavior.

Such extreme examples of greed and fraud may seem shocking. Yet how often, in our own environment, have we ignored, minimized, or accommodated questionable behavior to avoid confrontation or protect our own interests? How often have we turned a blind eye toward breaches of integrity? How often have we been less than authentic in our own communication? When added up throughout an organization,

1

such behaviors create costly corporate train wrecks. When added up throughout a society, the impact is even more devastating. Abuse of any nature—from simple lies to massive corporate fraud, from highway litter to rainforest destruction, from individual acts of bigotry to large-scale acts of terrorism—illustrates irresponsible, self-serving actions that negatively impact both the individual and the greater world.

As Bill George eloquently states in his highly acclaimed book, *Authentic Leadership: Rediscovering the Secrets to Creating Lasting Value*, "Somewhere along the way we lost sight of the imperative of selecting leaders that create healthy corporations for the long term. We need authentic leaders, people of the highest integrity, committed to building enduring organizations. We need leaders who have a deep sense of purpose and are true to their core values. We need leaders who have the courage to build their companies to meet the needs of all their shareholders, and who recognize the importance of their service to society." *The Leadership Integrity Challenge* addresses these very issues.

When integrity is missing, decline and decay are inevitable. The absence of integrity always precedes crises of character, vision, vitality, and human dignity. We can foretell the future of an individual, an organization, a society, or a culture by the values it prioritizes and upon which it acts. An entity with values and priorities based on the bedrock of integrity will thrive.

Integrity is much more than legal, moral, or social compliance. Clarifying what is acceptable behavior and obtaining agreement and compliance with those behaviors is often a needed first step. However, compliance actions, by themselves, do little to shift fundamental attitudes. We can spend a disproportionate amount of resources on the presenting problem rather than its cause. This is often the case when we are unclear on how to address and deal with the causal issue. Doing so virtually ensures that the problem will resurface and, like some viruses, morph into a more virulent form.

What we need, beyond clear communication and rules of

compliance to acceptable behavior, are programs that actually do facilitate an environment in which integrity is, in fact, the reality, not simply conforming to some socially acceptable norms. A vital aspect of these programs is the development of skills to better discern and differentiate those of integrity from the pretenders. To develop such programs, we need to understand the dynamics at a fundamental level. We must develop and use core competencies that address integrity itself, not just the symptoms of its lack.

To do so, it is helpful to observe a basic characteristic of integrity. Integrity is binary in nature; it is on or off. We may generally be people of integrity, but at any particular moment, we have it or we do not. Since development tends to be an accumulative process, how then, do we facilitate the development of integrity—and do so without imposing self-righteous judgments?

Even people who truly understand the vital importance of integrity often have little idea how to assess it, much less facilitate its development. Our culture itself tends to be a major inhibiting factor, tolerating and often promoting appearance over substance, too often at the expense of honesty and authenticity. Consequently, recognizing the difference between individuals of integrity and pretenders can be a real challenge. It's no wonder that leaders are honestly confused about how to evaluate and facilitate the development of integrity.

The key is to recognize the relationship between integrity and emotional maturity. Like the two strands in the double helix of our DNA, emotional maturity and integrity are inextricably interconnected. If a person is emotionally mature, he or she acts with integrity. If a person is emotionally immature, he or she will act irresponsibly and inevitably with a lack of integrity.

The fact is that most of us still have some growing up to do, some much more than others. As with integrity, we're either emotionally mature or we're not. However, with emotional maturity, we can distinguish relative degrees or levels of immaturity. By understanding these levels, we are able to assess our own and others' level of emotional maturity. From that understanding **we have the means to develop skills in facilitating movement toward greater emotional maturity**.

Daniel Goleman's groundbreaking book, *Emotional Intelligence*, brought greater public awareness to the importance and value of emotional intelligence. Developing our emotional intelligence can be a helpful and often necessary initial step toward facilitating emotional maturity. In addition, it is important to keep in mind that similar to cognitive intelligence, one may be emotionally intelligent yet have little real ability to apply that intelligence to the varying circumstances of life. That ability is the heart of, as well as the measure of, emotional maturity. Ultimately, developing and expanding our emotional maturity enables us to live more integral and fulfilled lives.

Facilitating the development of emotional intelligence and maturity (individually and organizationally) sets the all important framework for manifesting an emotionally mature environment of integrity, with all its strengths and benefits. The more emotionally mature an organization's employees, the more positive that organizations impact attracting more like-minded people of integrity.

The real leaders and change agents are those who set the tone and do what is necessary to ensure the development of a truly integrity-rich environment. **The most critical responsibility and long-term priority of enlightened leadership is to facilitate the development of emotional maturity.**

The purpose of this book is to assist in this noble challenge and adventure.

CHAPTER SUMMARIES

Chapter One: **Leadership—Making Change an Opportunity** addresses the issue of change and the role of leadership and emotional maturity in dealing with change. It defines and looks at the interrelationships of presence, responsibility, power, and empowerment. It reviews the dynamics and conditions that create or allow limiting and dysfunctional behavior.

Chapter Two: **The Emotionally Wise Leader** details the qualities and characteristics of emotionally wise leadership. It outlines and recommends a seven-step process to facilitate the development of emotional maturity and, thus, integrity. Suggestions to optimize training effectiveness are provided.

Chapter Three: **Integrity—The Vital Factor** provides greater clarity on the concept of integrity; indicates how it lays the foundation for vision, principals and character; stresses the costs of its lack and suggests how to put it into practice.

Chapter Four: **Emotional Intelligence and Beyond** looks at emotions, their meaning, and purpose and how we use and abuse them. It expands on the concept of emotional intelligence and acts as an emotional-intelligence primer for understanding emotional maturity.

Chapter Five: **Emotional Maturity** takes a deeper look at emotional maturity; what it is, why we so often act like self-centered children or self-important adolescents, and what we can do to start growing up

Chapter Six: **The Levels and Impact of Emotional Maturity** introduces the six levels of emotional maturity/immaturity, details the attitudes and behaviors of each level and shows how they can be used as a more objective measure in assessing emotional maturity.

Chapter Seven: **The Power of Communication** reviews some of the communication basics often forgotten but needed to translate convincingly the concept of emotional maturity into practical, achievable reality.

Chapter Eight: **Facilitating Emotional Maturity** is based on the emotional assessment tools presented in chapters 4, 5 and 6; this chapter develops the "how to" of facilitating individuals to higher levels of emotional maturity and integrity.

Epilogue: **A Call to Leadership**

1
Leadership—Making Change an Opportunity

You are not here merely to make a living. You are here in order to enable the world to live more amply, with greater vision, with a freer spirit of hope and achievement. You are here to enrich the world, and you impoverish yourself if you forget the errand. —Woodrow Wilson

"Outstanding!" Tom was ecstatic. He had just learned of his acceptance by the company that topped his wish list of potential employers. This company was recognized as a leader in its field. It had a reputation for being highly profitable, and paid excellent salaries. Its benefits program was exemplary. In addition, perhaps best of all, it was an easy commute. Tom was on cloud nine.

Alas, Tom discovered the internal climate at the company was not as portrayed. Almost immediately, he noticed a slew of seemingly arbitrary—and contradictory—directives sent, via email, from his division head. When he queried a colleague about it, the colleague told him it was not considered prudent to question the division head's judgment—on anything, "If you like working here," the colleague said, "you don't want to get on her bad side." It was also obvious that little meaningful communication existed among divisions or even between departments in the same division, making Tom's job particularly difficult. He was continually frustrated by so many individuals who were unwilling to share information.

After several months, Tom thought things might be improving when management assigned him to the company's Leadership

Development Program. The assignment was considered an excellent career-enhancement opportunity. However, he was soon disappointed to learn that the program's content and emphasis had little, if anything, to do with leadership. Rather, it was about how to ensure strict adherence to the company's historically very success-ful sales strategy.

People were not happy when Tom started questioning the truth-fulness of claims being made by the sales and marketing departments. Things went from bad to worse when he asked about some dubious financial arrangements. Tom's colleagues hinted rather strongly that his questions indicated a naiveté about how the "real world" operates. Increasingly he heard, "It's not an ideal world Tom, you have to be practical"; "Just do your job and let others worry about theirs"; and "You have a great job. Don't look a gift horse in the mouth." Unable to deny the obvious, Tom realized that management's touted open-door policy was a sham. Its values-based policy was a figment of the public relations department's imagination. Being a "good team member" seemed defined as not bringing up problems.

These were not isolated incidents. Tom concluded that manage-ment was alienating many employees, including key players, by cutting off feedback. To Tom, it was clear that current management policies were undermining the company's future. Quarterly sales and financial pressure precluded the needed changes from being consid-ered, much less implemented. Yet, management was not adapting to the changing competitive environment. Unless major changes were made, current profitability would not remain sustainable.

Tom loved the money he was making but he did not like what he was seeing or how it made him feel. He could not just ignore the problems, as some seemed to do, and was frustrated that he was not more personally effective. Those few people with whom he could share his concerns acknowledged the problem but felt as powerless as he.

Tom realized that the major problem the company was facing was not lack of salable products or technical skills. The people weren't bad but their unwillingness to confront issues on all management and employee levels did indicate a weakness of character. This translated into a lack of responsible action. Integral leadership was not one of the company's strong suits.

With growing alarm, Tom noticed that a number of the people he'd met when he started had moved on. He was not happy himself and knew he needed to start looking elsewhere, though he had some concerns about leaving: "How will leaving so soon look on my resume? Will I be able to land a job that is as well paying? Will I be able to handle the new mortgage payment? Why is it," Tom wondered, "that even when the need is obvious, change is so difficult?"

FACING THE CONFUSION, DOUBT AND FEAR OF CHANGE

When problems grow, demanding changes, will doing anything less than making those changes resolve the issue? The simple and obvious answer is no! Yet needed changes are continually avoided. Why? Because we are afraid. Real change means moving into the unknown. It means doing something different—it means not doing what is familiar or comfortable. It means not being able to rely on the old skills, connections, images, and pretenses that previously seemed to work. Change demands trying out new, often awkward, behaviors. It means being willing to let go of some old ways of being and doing. It means being vulnerable. Change is inherently threatening because there is always some degree of confusion, doubt and fear present, and—for those people being asked to change—there will always be some level of resistance.

Leadership is about persuading others to move beyond their comfort zone into the unknown. Creating substantive change therefore requires commitment—the willingness to face and persist through the predictable resistance that confusion, doubt and fear generate.

Without commitment, our desires and dreams remain little more than fantasy. Without integrity, there is no real commitment.

Too often, fearful, emotionally immature individuals and leaders are not willing to confront the predictable resistance to even desperately needed change. They claim that they will confront the resistance, but then they do not follow through. They're stymied by fear. For them, rationalizing a decision to stay with what is familiar feels much safer than facing their fears and dealing with the inevitable resistance to change.

The familiar may have been perfectly adequate and appropriate in the past, but may no longer be capable of doing the required job. Change will occur, but unless the discernment and flexibility of emotionally mature leadership is truly present, it is unlikely to be the change needed.

Emotionally mature people demonstrate responsible, flexible, resilient, and proactive behavior in the face of change. Emotionally immature people, out of fear and insecurity, reactively resist and fight change. Successful people are those who face their fears.

We must never lose time in vainly regretting the past nor in complaining about the changes which cause us discomfort, for change is the very essence of life. —Anatole France

Meaningful change requires a positive self-image, courage, and commitment, all of which are inherent to integrity. Without integrity, meaningful change is impossible. When real change is needed but ignored or only "fixes" are applied, what is missing is leadership.

SUBSTITUTING "FIXES" FOR LEADERSHIP
When emotional maturity and, thus, integrity and real leadership are lacking, needed change does *not* occur. Instead, a culture of resistance and rationalization develops.

Tremendous amounts of time and energy are spent on posturing, looking busy, protecting turf, and covering one's back. Personal values are compromised. Problems magnify. Some form of crisis is inevitable and will not be resolved by tweaking the system and returning to what is familiar and comfortable.

Improvement is an important aspect of being efficient, effective, and appropriate. Improvement is about making a good thing work better. "Fixes" are improvements to what is irrelevant or no longer doing the job that currently needs to be done. "Fixing" is a way to resist and avoid dealing with the difficult issues of real change.

Modifying or fixing what is no longer relevant and expecting it to work under the new conditions is like trying to protect the country by painting World War II fighter planes, giving them new engines, wheels, and controls, training pilots to fly them, and expecting them to survive dogfights with modern jet fighters. It is not only fuzzy thinking, but also very costly, deadly to the pilots, and a sure strategy for defeat.

Fixes are neither efficient nor effective. They squander time, money, material and, most of all, human capital. They are not only wasteful but can also be fatal, especially in a time of rapid change. Fixes deflect focus from what is actually needed. The fix may buy some time and thereby appease some political constituency, but it never lasts. If real change is needed, fixes only exacerbate the problem.

Fixes frustrate competent personnel and stifle innovation and creativity. They build up expectations that do not materialize, which, in turn, dashes hopes, creating even greater frustrations and, eventually, apathy. This makes it even more difficult for the next person in charge to gain support for needed changes when the crisis looms even larger. Implementing fixes is one of the surest ways to create mediocrity. If continued, they ensure the departure of the best and brightest.

Sometimes the existing paradigm needs reinforcement or development. Sometimes it needs breaking and replacing. The latter is usually the most difficult and resisted. Regardless, it takes wise leadership to

know which, when and how to do so. It takes the perspective and discernment of emotional maturity to distinguish among (1) fixing, (2) appropriate improvement and (3) the need for transformational change. To create transformational change, to stand tall and do what's right, takes guts.

REAL LEADERSHIP TAKES GUTS

Real leadership is about taking ourselves and others into new territory. It is about stretching old boundaries, trying the untried, taking risks, and being willing to fail. It takes courage to face the confusion, doubt, and fear that accompany any real change; to risk losing one's carefully crafted public image; and to persist through the inevitable resistance to any change. All of this boils down to our willingness to face our personal fears, which is what real courage is all about. Leadership takes guts, which means the willingness to face and deal with **whatever** is present.

Points to consider:

- What do you not want to confront? What decision or action are you avoiding?
- Whom are you avoiding?
- If you had the courage, what would you do to make your environment a better place?
- What part or aspect of that vision can you do now?

You have to have courage. I don't care how good a man is, if he is timid, his value is limited. —Theodore Roosevelt

PRESENCE—BEING IN THE MOMENT

Presence is the quality of being in **the now**, with full attention on and fully engaging the present environment, regardless of what that environment is. This is what Buddhists refer to as "mindfulness." Our ability to be present lays the foundation for discernment, which in turn makes it possible for us to respond effectively to whatever situations we face.

We can fully discern what is happening in the moment only when we are **in the now.** When we are not present, we miss information and lose discernment and thus limit our ability to make sound decisions; we cannot respond optimally. Being stuck in old patterns is a way of not being present. Unfortunately, it is a way that some people use to avoid dealing with a currently unpleasant situation responsibly. **Procrastination is an avoidance of being responsible NOW.**

The experience of being present with what is, is the experience of facing the truth. Any avoidance of experiencing what **is,** positive or negative, is an avoidance of the truth. Children and adolescents lie because they are afraid and insecure. Truly emotionally mature individuals have the awareness to know that real responsibility includes the willingness to face all truths.

Being emotionally mature means having the self-confidence and sense of security to deal with whatever a truth may be and to respond by taking positive action to the best of one's ability. As Eckhart Tolle points out in *The Power of Now*, it is our ability to be present with what is that is the foundation for our ability to respond and be truly powerful.

RESPONSIBILITY—THE ABILITY TO RESPOND

Responsibility is the ability to respond to and constructively deal with whatever is—the bad as well as the good. It should not be confused with social mores of expected behavior, which often have little relevance to what is occurring in the present but tend to be imposed as "responsible" behavior.

Responsibility is about becoming increasingly more self-referential. It is about each person honestly assessing and owning his or her unique part in creating or contributing to a situation and acting to make things better. It is about our willingness to be the source of our life. It incorporates the realization that everything we do, including what we choose to avoid, has impact. Responsibility is about owning and being accountable for that impact, and having the ability to respond (versus react) to the impact of forces outside of ourselves. It is being **response-able.**

Leadership is not rank, privilege, titles or money. Leadership is, ultimately, responsibility, and it's the ultimate responsibility.
—Colin Powell

Responsive Versus Reactive Behavior

Being responsive is being in the moment, being aware, and being able and willing to discern and differentiate relative priorities and take appropriate, constructive action. Responding is taking responsible action in the moment. **Responsive** individuals are those who listen and are willing and able to face and deal with whatever situation is at hand to the best of their ability, given the resources available. Only when one is responsive can one be responsibly proactive.

A **reactive** person is one who, in the past, was unable or unwilling to confront certain situations. Because the individual avoided the situations, they never resolved. They remained in place and, consequently, act like a magnet, keeping the individual's attention stuck in the past. To that extent, the individual is literally unable to observe, much less respond to, what is actually occurring in the present. As a result, the development of discernment and differentiation abilities is significantly limited.

With any additional avoidance, the stuffed energy accumulates, resulting in an increased feeling of overwhelm. For this reason, when people are reactive rather than responsive, their emotions and behaviors appear to be, and are, exaggerated relative to the present circumstances. They are reacting to the accumulated energy of the past, which the current situation often only re-stimulates. The greater the repression, the smaller the stimulus needed to create a reaction, the greater the reactivity, and the more hostile or despairing that reactivity will be. When a person is reactive, she cannot be, and will not be, responsibly proactive.

The outward attack that often accompanies reactivity is a projection of an individual's repressed feelings and his anger at himself for his unwillingness to take responsibility for his own behavior. The intensity of the attack (not necessarily the volume, for the attack can be covert and passive-aggressive) is an indication of the degree of repression, fear, and denial present with that individual.

As people feel overwhelmed, their willingness to take responsibility for their impact declines–exponentially. Truth becomes increasingly skewed and, depending on the extent to which a person feels overwhelmed, can become totally inverted. For example, when overwhelmed, what one person accuses another of is, sometimes literally, what he or she has done to the other person.

Any time we avoid being responsible, we automatically limit ourselves. The more we avoid responsibility, the more we allow ourselves to be controlled by things and circumstances "out there" and the greater is our sense of being powerless. We wind up acting like victims and become ineffective complainers.

The more personal responsibility we assume for our actions the more potential we have to direct toward achieving what we truly want. When responsible people find themselves feeling upset, they recognize that their feeling is a message that something's wrong. They quickly respond and transmute that upset energy into doing something constructive about the situation.

The flip side of responsibility is being judgmental and blaming. It is also doing something because one feels obligated. Responsibility viewed as a burden is not responsibility at all but a martyr's way of avoiding responsibility.

A man never describes his own character so clearly as when he describes another. —Jean Paul Richter

FALSE RESPONSIBILITY

A distortion of true responsibility is taking inappropriate responsibility for another person's actions or emotions. Helping other people help themselves is one thing. Taking responsibility for others, that is rescuing them, reinforces the message that they cannot handle the situation at hand. It is both arrogant and an invalidation of the other person.

Chronic rescuers feel they do not or will not have value unless they are rescuing someone. Therefore, they need someone to rescue and are very successful at creating needy relationships. This behavior inevitably leads to increased dependency, self-pity, victimhood, resentments, and mutual recriminations. It is what creates codependency, which is **always** debilitating and destructive to **all** parties.

Another form of false responsibility is using the mask and lie of being the "nice-guy." A nice-guy does not honestly confront others with their irresponsible actions, justifying that being honest might hurt their feelings or would not be gracious. However, those seemingly pleasant avoidances, more often than not, are little more than glib attempts to hide and excuse an unwillingness to face anything uncomfortable. The chronic nice-guys tend to have a limited inventory of what they think they can be, and a very large one of what they cannot or should not be. The nice-guys may avoid overt conflict and be more socially acceptable, but if successful, that behavior keeps them from dealing with their own fears and seeing their own hidden but inherent strengths and talents; in that process they deprive others of potentially valuable feedback. Consequently, their communication tends to be inauthentic and their promises untrustworthy.

Avoiding dealing with irresponsible behavior in the name of graciousness not only does nothing to end such behavior, but also it can actually reinforce it. This is especially true when people play the victim game of purposely trying to gain sympathy to deflect the negative consequence of their irresponsible behavior. It is a destructive game of manipulating and controlling through weakness. Allowing it to continue is disempowering to all parties.

As we recognize the vast difference between true gracious respect and superficial pleasantries to avoid dealing with certain issues, we open the door to experiencing and modeling greater presence and authenticity, thereby gaining effectiveness and respect. If we do not recognize and own the impact of **all** our behavior, we continually make ourselves the victim of forces outside of ourselves and feel more and more out of control and powerless.

Points to consider:

- **How often do you offer to help someone?**
- **When you do, what is your usual motive for doing so?**

POWER—THE ABILITY AND THE WILLINGNESS TO ACT

Power is both the ability and the willingness to act. Ability without willingness to use it generates nothing. Likewise, willingness without ability has no power. Both ability and willingness must be present.

Power is a potential; it is not an action itself. That is why powerful people seldom have to actually demonstrate their power. Their recognized willingness and ability to act often is all that's needed to get the desired response.

Power stems from an ability to hold a position. Try pushing a heavy object while standing on a patch of ice—you have no solid position from which to establish traction. Similarly, when a person is insecure, frightened, overwhelmed, or has low self-esteem, there is no solid foundation from which to generate anything.

Real power is based on an individual's fundamental sense of security and positive self-esteem. It is not conditional on anyone else's actions or approval. People who are secure do not need to resort to threats or manipulation; insecure people often do.

True power has nothing to do with intimidation or manipulation. Would-be leaders use various forms of intimidation, manipulation and invalidation to hide their insecurity and force others into fear or apathy. The only power they have is the power we allow them.

Repressive behaviors are manifestations and symptoms of false power, of a perceived need to have power and control over someone or something as compensation for a lack of real power and a feeling of being out of control. Because false power is based in insecurity, it has no substantive foundation and thus usually collapses if responsibly confronted. In the meantime, it can do a lot of damage.

Real power, like integrity and presence, is totally individual and demands a personal willingness and ability to be responsible. Responsibility is integral to power, for only with the ability to respond to what is, do we have the ability to constructively act. Any irresponsible behavior is an indication of a lack of real power. Correspondingly, increased responsibility always creates increased power.

Points to consider:

- What are you unable to do that you say you want to do?
- How willing are you to do what's necessary to develop that ability?
- What do you refuse to do?
- Is your refusal based on ethical principles or because you are afraid?

EMPOWERMENT—GIVING YOURSELF PERMISSION TO ACT

As power is about potential, empowerment is about manifesting that potential. The key is to giving ourselves the permission and assuming the authority (owning our authorship) to act. As with power, both aspects—permission and authority—must be present. If we do not give ourselves permission to act, we cannot do anything, regardless of the potential available. When we deny our authorship, that is, our part in either creating or allowing the situation, we forgo any authority to change the script. Empowerment is the direct result of our willingness to take responsibility and be accountable for the impact we have.

People speak of empowering others. However, true empowerment is not and cannot be given by some other person or entity. It can only be given to ourselves, by ourselves. Only we can give ourselves the permission and assume the authority of our action or inaction (our impact). Others can only provide a supportive (or not) environment. **Developing that environment is a vital element to organizational success and longevity. Its presence is a measure of truly effective leadership.**

The key to self-empowerment is to first own the truth of the following statements:

- Whatever we do (or do not do) has impact;
- We create or allow our reality;
- We reinforce that which we give our attention.

The degree to which we allow, own, and actualize these points is the degree to which we build a foundation for empowerment. Realize that whenever we find ourselves reacting (feeling put upon, upset, or blaming) rather than responding (dealing with a situation constructively), we are denying that we have impact and, instead, we are directing all focus outside of ourselves. In others words, we are giving power away and focusing our attention on how the external world has victimized us. This reinforces a disempowering perception. However, because we do have impact, we have contributed at least something to the existing reality. Therefore, that perception cannot be valid. In this sense, there are no victims, only volunteers.

Points to consider:

- **Name something specific that you are not doing that you would feel good about doing.**
- **Is there any reason you cannot possibly do it?**
- **What is stopping you?**

- Are you stopping yourself?
- Consider taking your "stop" off and give yourself permission to start—if you really want to. What would be your first step?
- It is your creation; acknowledge your authorship—if you are willing. How will you begin your next chapter?

A good leader inspires one to have confidence in him; a great leader inspires them to have confidence in themselves. —Sun Tzu

GOALS—AN ANCHOR TO THE FUTURE

Having clear goals sets an anchor into the future, providing a focus and helping to keep one from wandering aimlessly, wasting time and resources. To the degree that people are unclear about personal goals, they will have difficulty relating to and being motivated by organizational goals, even if the latter are clearly stated. There is little basis for alignment. With no perceived alignment, there will be frustration, upset, and generalized complaints. If, for whatever reasons, organizational goals are unclear, people with focused personal goals are more likely to be creative and responsible in helping to clarify organizational goals and aligning them with their own. To align personal, professional, and organizational goals, it's best to do the following:

1. Focus on and clarify personal goals;
2. Focus on and clarify professional goals;
3. Clarify and focus on organizational goals.

Organizational results tend to be optimized to the degree the above steps are (1) all given respectful attention; (2) addressed in the above sequence with personal goals first, professional goals second, and then organizational goals; and (3) in alignment with and supportive of one another.

All must be in alignment, mutually supporting, and in balance. When the balance is lost, optimal performance will not be attained.

More often than not, this sequence and emphasis is violated, with organizational goals receiving dominant attention at the expense of individual aspirations. When that occurs, the individual tends to become frustrated and distracted. The cost, to both the individual and the organization, can be huge.

Points to consider:
- Are your needs and aspirations being addressed?
- Have you clarified, for yourself, what they are?
- How can you responsibly make sure you are addressing them?
- How can you align your needs in a way that contributes to an organization's well-being?
- What, specifically, can you do?
- Are you willing to do it? If not, why not?

The tragedy of life doesn't lie in not reaching your goal. The tragedy lies in having no goal to reach. —Benjamin Mays

I cannot commend to a business house any artificial plan for making men producers—any scheme for driving them into business-building. You must lead them through their self-interest. It is this alone that will keep them keyed up to the full capacity of their productiveness.

—Charles H. Steinway

BUTCHER, BAKER, CANDLESTICK MAKER— WHEN ARE YOU WHICH?

Every position in an organization requires and makes use of multiple and different skill sets. There are times when we need to use our technical skills. There are times when we need to manage, and there are times we need to lead. This is true for anyone and everyone in the organization, regardless of title or position.

However, it is important to differentiate the skill sets and know when each is required in the moment. It is important not to confuse leadership with management. Managers deal with what already exists. Leadership is about breaking ground—it is about motivating others to unexplored heights and new territories.

Honestly look at yourself and what you do in your current job. Each job has its place, but different functions and different responsibilities are needed at different times.

Points to consider:

- To what degree are you a leader, a manager, or a technician?
- When are you which?
- Are you being a technician when you should be managing, or otherwise enacting one role when you should be fulfilling another?
- You may find yourself doing what is familiar or what you are good at, but are they what you need to do now?
- It may be useful, but is it a top priority now?
- Which functions or subjects do you tend to avoid or feel uncomfortable?
- What could you be doing that might be of even bigger benefit to both you and the organization? Why aren't you doing it?

OBSTACLES TO CHANGE
Over-managed and Under-led

Former head of the Strategic Air Command, General Jack Chain, continually emphasized, "You lead people and manage things." Yet how often has this been confused or abused—the too common result being that we wind up treating people like things that need to be managed rather than individuals who need to be motivated by competent leadership?

We live in a world that, with rare exception, rewards managers but avoids developing leaders. Why? Managing, for the most part, is about ensuring that what needs to be done is done within an existing system— a familiar system. Good management requires an understanding of the existing system and keeping it efficient and effective. Leadership is about getting others to move beyond the familiar. When people actually lead, they upset the old, familiar system and its vested interests. Managing the familiar tends to be much less threatening than leading people into an unknown and much less predictable future.

Both managing and leading require many of the same underlying skills and qualities—for example, good communication, emotional intelligence, and emotional maturity. However, competent leadership demands an additional ability to stretch boundaries and overcome fears.

Points to consider:

- How often do you stretch boundaries?
- Are you encouraged and supported in doing so?
- Do you over-manage and under-lead?
- What problems concern you?
- To whom can you communicate your concerns?

The "We're Successful" Syndrome

If an organization's leadership becomes enamored with the success of what has worked, particularly their own success within that structure, they can become emotionally dependent on its retention, blind themselves to the needs of an evolving environment, and rationalize their resistance to any substantive change. "Look at how successful we are. We want people who can make the existing system even better. We don't want people upsetting a proven success formula."

When the latter viewpoint prevails, true leadership development is effectively disallowed. Though programs may retain the title of leadership development, what is allowed and offered instead are programs limited to management (not leadership) development. The effective impact of this restricted (and often misleading) focus is that the adaptability and innovation needed for sustainability decline.

Sustainability, especially in a competitive environment, depends on keeping an effective balance between managing a working system and leading it into new arenas. In a dynamic environment, that balance is critical. Lack of balance always shows up in failed or declining organizations. Unless that dynamic balance is reestablished, organizational success predictably becomes history rather than an ongoing current event. An organization caught in the "We're Successful" syndrome requires the courage of true leadership, not solely the skills of well-rewarded managers doing what worked before.

Points to consider:

- **What is your organization doing simply because it worked in the past?**
- **In what ways has your organization been exploring new frontiers, innovating, and taking risks?**

In times of change, those who are ready to learn will inherit the world, while those who believe they know will be marvelously prepared to deal with a world that has ceased to exist. —Eric Hoffer

"Their Numbers Are Up"

How often do we see obviously dysfunctional, emotionally immature people maintain their position and even be rewarded or promoted because their financial numbers are up? Mature leadership expects that positive, appropriate results be achieved. The viability of an enterprise depends on it. Numbers are a way to measure those results. They can be very helpful—if the appropriate measures are used.

Organizations are complex, and it can be helpful to simplify the measures to expedite decisions and actions. However, especially when short-term financial or political factors play a significant role, the numbers are sometimes reduced to one or a few figures. Important factors that constitute real productivity and have long-term implications are often ignored or rationalized away. When that occurs chronically, the results are an inefficient use of resources, repressed communication, frustration, decreased morale, and the eventual loss of the best and the brightest.

When a dysfunctional executive's figures are up, more often than not, those figures are not valid indicators of real productivity. The positive results that are valid are more likely to be despite the person's actions, not because of them. When an obviously dysfunctional executive is kept in place because his numbers are up, something is being denied or ignored. It is a sure sign of weak leadership—ignorant of or unwilling or unable to deal with what needs to be confronted.

Points to consider:

- **How careful do you need to be in discussing topics like this in your workplace?**
- **Have you ever mistaken an upswing in your financial numbers for success?**
- **Beside the numbers, what other indicators help you to determine if what you are doing is effective and successful?**

Mind Reading Required

How often do we see authenticity replaced with partial truths or outright lies? To what degree is one expected to read between the lines of most communication? How often have we been kept on hold waiting for a decision that had already been made but was intentionally not communicated?

Communication of this type occurs continually in organizations. It always results in frustrations, inefficiencies, and loss of trust. The degree to which lack of honesty and authenticity is condoned, encouraged, allowed, or not confronted is a direct indication of the level of leadership immaturity and the lack of integrity (which is always rationalized).

Points to consider:

- How would you describe the quality of your immediate group's communication?
- How authentically does your supervisor communicate?
- How authentic is your communication with your supervisor, peers, subordinates, and family members?
- Are misleading or meaningless communications the norm?
- How have you dealt with this type of situation in the past?

"But I Intended to Do It"

Intention is a necessary precursor to results, especially when you are trying to initiate change. Try to do something—for example, get out of your chair, without intending to do so. You can't do it. Conscious or unconscious, it is our intention that is fundamental to what we allow to happen in our perception of reality.

If we are willing to look, we can have a reliable means to understand anyone's actual intention(s) (including our own), by observing what she (or we) actually winds up doing. What intention would someone need to create that result? For example, Judy was supposed to accomplish X. Instead, Y occurred. She says, "But I really intended to do X." That statement is simply not true. She got Y. Therefore, at some level, conscious or unconscious, her intent was Y not X—or the Y intention was stronger and overrode the X intention. She may have consciously wanted to do X but unconsciously had a stronger intention to do Y.

If someone is having difficulty executing what he needs to do, particularly when he supposedly has the skills to do so, look to his intention. The motive will be different than claimed. Behind the actual intention, conscious or unconscious, will be some emotion upon which the person is fixated. It is usually hostility (overt or covert), fear (real or imagined), grief (stuck in some loss), or apathy (why bother). All are various symptoms and degrees of feeling overwhelmed.

If an individual is exhibiting any dysfunctional symptoms, simple observation will show a person in some degree of overwhelm. That person is feeling insecure, but often pretending otherwise. The dysfunctional behavior is a manifestation of some self-sabotaging intention and belief (again conscious or unconscious). Addressing the symptoms, that is, the behavior, will not provide more than temporary relief. The underlying intention needs to be brought to light and its motivation recognized, acknowledged (owned), and addressed. *The Power of Intention*, by Wayne Dyer, develops the importance of this dynamic in detail.

Points to consider:

- **Think of an instance when your stated intention was different from your results. Are you aware of what your actual intention was?**
- **What were you reluctant to communicate, acknowledge, address, or confront?**

The Genesis of Crazy-Making

In studying schizophrenic behavior, Dr. Gregory Bateson observed that a person's mental state appeared to be much more dependent on the interaction between the individual and his or her environment than it was on what was going on with his or her internal mental processes. With that observation, Bateson wanted to determine the kind of environment that could or would trigger schizophrenic behavior.

Based on additional studies, Bateson developed the theory of the Double Bind, a process and set of conditions that tend to create schizophrenic behavior. Drs. Chris Argyris and Donald Schön did a parallel study of organizations and observed an almost identical process and set of conditions that result in schizophrenic behavior. That process and those conditions are the following:

1. Have someone with authority over another;

2. The person with authority gives a direction or order to the subordinate, along with some threat (implicit or explicit) of negative consequences for noncompliance. Example: "If you want a promotion, make sure I know everything that's going on!";

3. The authority then gives a contradictory instruction, also with some threat. Example: "You're always telling me the problems. I want solutions, not problems. You had better start getting it right!"

This creates the "Double Bind," that is, "Damned if I do, damned if I don't." The following are what make the Double Bind crazy-making:

1. The authority makes the contradiction undiscussable, and includes some form of threat. Example: "What contradictions? You're creating problems where there are none!";

2. The authority makes the undiscussability undiscussable but pretends it is not. Example: "What do you mean we can't talk about it?! You know I have an open-door policy on everything! I'm becoming quite concerned about your management potential here.";

3. The authority ensures that the other person feels he or she cannot leave the situation. Example: For senior executives, this deterrent may be in the form of "golden handcuffs." For others, it may simply be a tight labor market or concerns about a negative reference.

The most troubling aspect is not the contradictions but their undiscussability. Opening the door to resolution demands an honest assessment of one's own role in a situation and a willingness to discuss contradictions. Most troubling is not that an organization has contradictions, but that the contradictions are often undiscussed or, worse, undiscussable.

"Schizophrenergetic" (crazy-making) behavior is more prevalent in organizations than most people realize or are willing to acknowledge. It significantly reduces the likelihood of implementing needed change. This is particularly true in times of increased stress. How do we stay sane and responsibly proactive in complex environments which can, naively or not, create schizophrenergetic behavior? Crazy-making environments can be righted if competent communication skills and willingness to dialogue are present. One of the most important things we can do is recognize how we may be contributing to schizophrenergetic behavior. If you observe crazy-making behavior ask yourself, "How am I either creating or contributing to this situation?"

The "Silo Effect"

How often do we observe a lack of communication and interaction among groups in the same organization? This isolating behavior, known as the **silo effect,** severely limits potential synergies of strategic and functional alignment. The loss of cross selling opportunities among departments and divisions is but one example.

The reasons for this lack of communication can range from simple introversion into assigned tasks to significant turf issues. Regardless, the silo effect is the manifestation of some avoidance of responsibility. The basis is always some real or imagined fear. This must be brought to light and dealt with or the organization will not capitalize on its potential. The degree to which the silo effect is a chronic condition is a direct indication of insecure, apathetic, arrogant, or incompetent management and leadership. If present, it needs priority attention.

Well-designed and well-delivered communication programs and competent coaching can be very helpful in relieving the silo effect, as can the *Communication Clearing Process* outlined in Chapter 7, page 188. However, all will be for naught if people are afraid to speak their truth. The presence or absence of a safe environment where honest communication and true dialogue can flourish is a direct reflection of what senior management actually wants and is willing to allow.

The presence of spontaneous, authentic communication is an indication that senior management is relatively secure and has a healthy sense of self-confidence and self-esteem. That indication of emotional maturity at the top suggests a positive prognosis for the organization as a whole.

The willingness and ability to honestly confront repressed communication has a more significant impact on organizational effectiveness than personal charisma, management style, incentive programs, technical expertise, or product uniqueness. Those can be valuable, sometimes vital, but they will not be capitalized on to the extent possible if repressed communication—of any nature—is present.

When the silo effect is eliminated or even lessened, synergies occur, and both productivity and morale rise, often dramatically. Effectively dealing with the silo effect or, for that matter, any communication deficiency, should be a senior priority of management.

Points to consider:
- How prevalent is the silo effect in your organization?
- Between which groups is it most noticeable?
- How would you evaluate the effectiveness of those groups' management?
- If you were CEO, what would you do?

ALLEVIATE THE NUMBERS GAME

No one will deny that a leader's job is to ensure an organization's growth and development. No one will deny that to be sustainable, an organization needs to show a return on its resources. Nor will they deny that how that is done needs to be accurately communicated to its stakeholders.

Nevertheless, most will agree and that the current corporate financial reporting process is dysfunctional. Its short-term emphasis misallocates resources that often have costly long-term consequences. Perhaps even more significant, it breeds dishonesty, manipulation and fraud.

So, how can corporate leaders move beyond the "numbers game?" They can by communicating to the investment community the factors that drive long-term value in their companies. New York University Professor Baruch Lev of the Stern School of Business states that more than half of the market value of S&P 500 companies is due to non-financial factors. Some of these are quality of management, execution of corporate strategy, corporate reputation and brand, innovation in developing new products or services, research and development efforts, patents, use of human and intellectual capital, and alliances and business relationships.

These non-financial factors are more difficult to measure. For many, it is easier to hang one's hat on quarterly financials than to do the needed work of providing a more comprehensive (and honest) perspective. This is misleading and incomplete and therefore lacks integrity. By focusing communication on balancing financial and non-financial factors, leaders can move the discussion of their companies away from the short-term toward a more balanced perspective of the actual factors that drive value for the long term.

We need leaders who are willing to stand tall, be creative, insist on and model a new forthright, balanced process. From that example, we all can learn and together co-create a new standard of integral reporting that better serves all stakeholders. **Where are these paradigm-shifting heroes?**

THE DNA OF A FULFILLED LIFE

2
The Emotionally Wise Leader

To live in the company of Men-at-their-best is the finest thing possible. How can a man be considered wise, if when he has the choice, he does not live in such surroundings? —Confucius

THE EMOTIONALLY WISE LEADER—
QUALITIES AND CHARACTERISTICS

The previous chapter looked at the difficulty people and organizations have in dealing with even vitally needed change. It briefly described some of the more common issues that arise and suggested that we would be better served by the presence of a more emotionally mature population.

This chapter looks at the characteristics of emotionally wise leadership and outlines a process to facilitate the development of an emotionally mature organization built on integrity. It also addresses training concerns that, when addressed, help to optimize the developmental process and impact. Subsequent chapters clarify and develop specific aspects of that process.

The maturity of an organization's leadership is what sets the tone for everything that follows. It creates the environment that determines the organization's values and its contribution to the world.

Emotionally wise leaders share certain qualities and characteristics:

- They do not repress feelings, but rather express and use them in ways that positively contributes;

- They live and consciously relate and act from fundamental core values;
- They have a sense of purpose. Their contribution extends beyond themselves;
- They authentically walk their talk. They are willing to share their ideas and feelings with honesty, sincerity, sensitivity, and compassion;
- They have presence. They listen and acknowledge others;
- They have a healthy sense of perspective and balance;
- They can see the big picture without losing sight of the current situation;
- They are responsive to their environment rather than reactive to it;
- They are aware that everything they do and say has impact, and they are responsible and accountable for that impact;
- When that impact is not the result they want, they have the flexibility and resiliency to change their behavior;
- They are willing to honestly look at themselves and acknowledge both their shortcomings and their strengths;
- They have the discipline, determination, and persistence to correct their shortcomings, expand current strengths, and develop other strengths;
- They are secure in themselves. They are willing to ask for and receive help. They are willing to let someone else take charge if that person can do a better job;
- They have the capability and willingness to develop intimate and lasting relationships;
- They do not, and will not, tolerate irresponsible or unethical behavior;
- They help others help themselves;
- They encourage, develop, and facilitate dialogue;
- They have sensitivity and respect for the dignity of all with

whom they come into contact and, thus, create an
environment in which individuals are respected for
who they are and feel safe to expand and grow;

- They have well-defined and clearly communicated
  boundaries of behavior (principles);
- They have character, vision, and vitality;
- They are able to assess and evaluate relative priorities, allowing them to make sane decisions and to act with both
  humility and a sense of confidence, even under
  difficult or rapidly changing circumstances;
- They are adaptable and know which role to play when;
- They are trustworthy, and they trust people who have
  earned their trust;
- They have the courage to try new things, make mistakes,
  and learn from them;
- They have the determination to deal with and persevere
  through the inevitable resistance (their own as well as
  that of others) to real change;
- Above all, they have integrity. Integrity is the core of truly
  great leadership and is developed in depth in Chapter 3.

These are the qualities and characteristics that correlate to
organizational success and long-term maximization of profits. They are
characteristics extolled but seldom consistently observed.

Emotional maturity is the foundation that provides the emotionally wise leader with the presence, confidence, flexibility, and
willingness to confront what needs to be faced. This foundation
enables him to see the big picture; make strategic decisions, changes,
and commitments; innovate, execute, follow through and get the
desired results, all with sensitivity and compassion. It is the demonstra-
tion of these qualities that enables the emotionally wise leader to
inspire commitment and action from others in ways that contribute to

the expanded well-being and awareness of others. Inspiring that commitment is, after all, the real measure of leadership.

These qualities provide a competitive advantage. They are only consistent and persistent with emotionally mature individuals of integrity. Thus, emotional maturity is itself a competitive advantage, and it lays a solid foundation for generating additional competitive advantages.

Leadership style and method among individuals can and does vary considerably. Those who consciously live with such qualities and behavior cannot help but be responsible leaders who get productive results. They are the emotionally wise leaders. This does not mean they have perfect judgment or do not make mistakes. They make plenty of mistakes but seldom repeat the same ones, because they consciously make a point to learn from each one.

Emotionally wise leaders realize they are living in a dynamic universe. Survival itself depends on one's ability and willingness to work with that dynamic rather than fight or resist it. Therefore, emotionally wise leaders naturally are innovative and creative. They easily step where others fear to tread.

Emotionally wise leaders are the ones who act on this awareness. They know that key to organizational emotional maturity and, thus, to an organization's vitalization is the selection of people who have the greatest potential of making a positive contribution. They realize that hiring, developing, and supporting emotionally mature people of integrity should be among their primary strategies and policies. They look for and proactively facilitate the development of emotional maturity in others. Whatever form it takes, their priority is to create an emotionally mature organization of integrity. They are willing to do, with integrity, whatever it takes to achieve that.

Points to consider:

- **What is your top priority for the next year (hint: To what do you give most of your attention)?**

- On your list of priorities, how far from the top is the development of emotional maturity? Honestly, is it a real priority at all?
- Are you so busy with other things that you just don't have the time to work on emotional maturity?
- If so, how long has this been going on?
- Given your organization, if you were CEO and wanted to create a profitable, sustainable, and integral organization with high morale and an outstanding reputation, what would be your priorities and their order of importance?
- What would be your first action?

Example is not the main thing in influencing others. It's the only thing.
—Albert Schweitzer

SELECTING, DEVELOPING AND RETAINING EMOTIONALLY MATURE PEOPLE

Key to personal, organizational, and leadership development and vitalization is the selection and retention of individuals who have the greatest potential for making a positive contribution. Emotionally mature individuals are most capable and most likely to optimally use inherent talents and maximally develop needed functional skills, even if those skills are not initially present. They are the most mentally and emotionally present and, therefore, the most capable of meeting their own needs and the needs of clients and the organization.

Emotionally mature people of integrity have a strong and real sense of self-worth. Being emotionally secure, they are willing to learn and are open to new ideas and opportunities. Their perspective is broad and balanced. This has a direct impact on their potential for real contribution and happiness. The more emotionally mature people of integrity there are in an organization, the more positive that impact.

When leadership is weak, we notice certain out-of-proportion tendencies. Personnel selections tend to be almost entirely based on factors other than integrity and emotional maturity. This can range, for example, from hiring only yes-men to a sole emphasis on hiring people with a certain functional expertise. Functional competence and experience are vital to organizational success. However, they are secondary to emotional maturity and integrity. Emotionally mature individuals are secure about themselves and therefore have little need to defend ideas or positions. These individuals tend to be responsible and adaptive, easily learning what needs to be done. **Placing little real attention on integrity and emotional maturity is one of the costliest, yet most common, mistakes of many executives.**

In terms of optimizing both results and return on investment, whom to send to training can be a critical determination. Training programs that are well-designed, competently delivered, and appropriately reinforced can and do have a very positive impact—when delivered to emotionally mature people.

Unfortunately, management often selects personnel for development programs based on job title or function rather than emotional maturity. Because emotionally immature individuals are feeling overwhelmed, they are reactive rather than responsive. Their defensive reaction precludes being open to new ideas and, thus, to change and growth. Therefore, most training for the emotionally immature is more often than not a waste of resources.

Retaining emotionally immature individuals is always both costly and hurtful. Keeping such people in place is costly to the organization, because emotional immaturity always diverts resources—mental, emotional, or physical. It is hurtful to the individuals, because it protects them from facing their immaturity by supporting dysfunctional behaviors.

Only by attracting the best people will you accomplish great deeds.
—Colin Powell

VITALIZING THE ORGANIZATION
AND OPTIMIZING PERFORMANCE

The presence of integrity and emotional maturity is foundational and vital to optimizing an organization's real performance and long-term success. This cannot be emphasized strongly enough. It is from that foundation that all things flow. Therefore, the first priority of leadership is to evaluate the emotional maturity of its senior staff, as those individuals set the tone and resonance for all people under them. Since like attracts like, these people will draw in and select those who are of a comparable emotional level.

Despite the profound impact of integrity, many leaders focus their attention and energy elsewhere. This is not to minimize other important areas of leadership responsibility. However, more than most people realize, a lack of attention on the importance of integrity effectively results in a tremendous waste of human potential. It takes a huge toll on individual dignity and morale and has enormous financial and environmental costs. Authenticity and honest communication are some of the first things to suffer. We often ignore or fail to recognize that our integrity or the lack thereof, has a direct impact on our self-image, self-respect, self-esteem, and self-confidence. Our integrity profoundly affects our actions, our feelings, our relationships, our results, and our happiness.

Lack of integrity inevitably creates problems. But, without addressing causal factors, the actual—and potential—problems do not and will not go away. They only magnify. Seemingly every decade or two, the corporate business world explodes into a rash of scandals, creating a flurry of finger pointing, blame, and demands for tougher laws. These explosions recur largely because, as problems become apparent, we do nothing or, in our attempts to do something, devote our efforts primarily toward dealing with symptoms. When we do so, often we do not recognize, much less address, the underlying cause or causes.

For example, in response to recent scandals, passing new laws or clarifying and requiring adherence to expected behaviors may be helpful, even necessary, initial steps. However, those expected behaviors must align with the individual's fundamental values. There also needs to be present a sense of personal ownership. If these are not present, the result will be, predictably, little more than social compliance with no "juice." Without real ownership, compliance begins to wane and more outside enforcement mechanisms are needed. Clarifying what is expected is a positive step and may address some legal and public relations concerns. However, complying with someone else's standard is not what constitutes or creates integrity.

The following outlines a process to expand higher levels of emotional maturity and integrity and, thus, organizational vitalization, growth, and performance.

THE RECOMMENDED PROCESS
Step I. Secure Management Commitment

Ensure senior management believes in and is committed to the primacy of integrity and emotional maturity in all organizational processes. This includes relationships outside the organization as well as selecting, hiring, developing, promoting, and retaining people within the organization. When this commitment to organizational integrity and emotional maturity is truly present, the positive resonance and energy of the entire organization necessarily rises—often dramatically so. **Management's commitment itself must have integrity, that is, it must be authentic and complete.** Anything less will be misleading and result in fostering cynicism, misallocating resources, and undermining leadership credibility. This commitment must be communicated, nurtured, developed, attained and supported throughout the entire organization. (See A *Word of Caution: The Impact of Self-Image*, this chapter, page 49.)

A cup of water to put out a cartload of burning firewood is an inadequate response. —Chinese saying

Note: The following Steps II and III should be concurrently implemented for maximum effectiveness. Subsequent chapters are devoted primarily to developing the clarity, models, and means to facilitate these two steps.

Step II. Educate the Organization

Integrity and emotional maturity are qualities that have a fundamental impact on everything we think, feel, and do. If an organization truly intends to revitalize itself with integrity and emotional maturity as its foundation, then everyone in the organization needs to understand the following:

- What emotional maturity and integrity actually are and their interrelationship;
- Their vital importance;
- Management's commitment to developing an emotionally mature organization of integrity;
- How to evaluate integrity and emotional maturity;
- How to facilitate the development of emotional maturity, personally, professionally and organizationally.

It's not enough to do your best. You must know what to do and then do your best. —W. Edwards Deming

Step III. Facilitate Individuals to Empower Themselves

III-a.) Develop presence. Presence, as discussed in Chapter 1, is the quality of being in the **now**, with full attention on and fully engaging the present environment regardless of what that environment is. It is "mindfulness." Our presence is the foundation of our discernment, upon which our integrity stands. It is the platform for personal power.

When we are mentally or emotionally distracted, we miss information, lose discernment, and limit our facility for decision making. The result is a less-than-optimal response. Being stuck in old patterns is not being present. To the degree we are stuck, we cannot and will not act responsibly.

Responsibility is a component of and integral to true power. Without presence, which gives us the possibility of acting responsibly, we cannot be operating with integrity or be truly powerful. Our ability to be present is the foundation of our integrity and personal power.

Treat people as if they were what they ought to be and you will help them to become what they are capable of being.
—Johann Wolfgang von Goethe

III-b.) Eliminate repressed communication. Repressed communication is the bane of most organizations and is a major cause of the "silo effect" so common within organizations. The willingness and ability to honestly confront repressed communication has a tremendous impact on leadership and organizational effectiveness. Other positive qualities and virtues may exist in an organization, but they will not be fully realized as long as communication is repressed.

There is a direct connection between the degree of repressed communication and the degree of emotional immaturity in a person or an organization. The degree to which repressed communication is released is the degree to which co-creation, real collaboration, and true teamwork can manifest. This, in turn, expands creativity, innovation, efficiency, effectiveness, productivity, customer relations, and cross-selling. This impacts morale, turnover, profitability and sustainability. The *Communication Clearing Process* outlined in Chapter 7, page 188, can be very helpful in initially facilitating more open communication. However, the most important influencing factor is the communication modeled by the organization's leadership.

III-c.) Find and transform limiting beliefs and self-sabotaging patterns. Fortunately, recent advances in energy psychology have made finding and transforming limiting beliefs a relatively easy process. Of particular note in this arena is the work of Andrew Hahn, Psy.D. He has developed an innovative process that elegantly finds and transforms the original cause of the problem including limiting beliefs. His book, *Guided Self Healing* will be available in 2006.

In *Power Versus Force*, David Hawkins, M.D., Ph.D. evaluates relative states of awareness and real contribution from a macro perspective. His research points out that even a few people of integrity not hindered by limiting beliefs can have an enormous influence in shaping our world.

III-d.) Develop a positive self-image. Self-image sets the boundary of what a person is capable. If we expand our self-image, we expand our ability and willingness to co-create and contribute. We can enhance our self-image, but only if we are willing to look honestly at ourselves. Most people, unfortunately, are too insecure to do that. Our goal is to create and be part of an organization where honest self-assessment is the norm.

In addition to Step III-c, *The Self-Image Process*, outlined in Chapter 7, page 189, can be a useful (and sometimes profound) process for significantly expanding a person's real self-image. But it cannot be done glibly; if it is, it's a waste of time.

III-e.) Help the able be more able. Recognize and develop individual underlying strengths, inherent talents, and hidden or repressed passions. Along with selecting emotionally mature individuals and providing programs to eliminate repressed communication, we must encourage an organization to provide an environment that nurtures individual development. A leadership that truly wants the organization to grow and capitalize on its full potential cannot afford to ignore individual development. For an organization comprised of the emotionally mature, this is not a problem, because those individuals will create such an environment. They proactively do the following:

- Help individuals recognize, determine, and uncover their own values and unique strengths and talents. When those are found, passion follows. (See *The Value of Competent Coaching*, Chapter 8, page 205);

- Place individuals in jobs and on assignments where their talents and proclivities can be best used, encouraged, and developed. Focus on building from individual unique strengths. *People Pattern Power: The Nine Keys to Business Success* by Wyatt and Marilyne Woodsmall, provides methods to easily assess individual proclivities and optimally align them with varying functional skill needs;

- Assist individuals who are not performing up to their full potential and do not delay in removing and replacing individuals who are unwilling to change. (See *Willingness– The Determining Factor*, Chapter 5, page 126);

- Provide or demand competent facilitation, coaching and training, as needed, for personal, professional and organizational growth.

Everyone has talent. What is rare is to recognize it and then have the courage to follow the talent to the unknown place where it might lead.
—Sandra Day O'Connor

Step IV. Co-create the Organization's Vision, Core Values, Strategic Intent, Strategic Objectives and Operating Principles

Without co-creation, the best an organization's leadership can ever expect is willing compliance—a far less motivating energy. Co-creation provides an individual with a feeling of involvement, participation, and contribution, greatly increasing his or her sense of determination, commitment and ownership. Some call this energy passion; some call it heart. The degree of co-creation and heart energy present relates directly to the level of emotional maturity present. The higher that level, the greater an individual's:

1. Fundamental sense of security;
2. Ability to let go of what is no longer working;
3. Openness to consider different opinions and options;
4. Ability to authentically dialogue;
5. Willingness to stretch into the unknown.

A group of individuals collaborating from this foundation generates a world of exciting possibilities previously considered impossible. Recognize that the co-creative process will be a sham to the degree emotional maturity and Steps I-III above are glossed over or rationalized away.

An organization's **vision** provides a picture of the ideal. The emotional maturity and integrity present within the organization determine not only how big and how compelling the organization's vision will be, but also the probability that the vision will be manifested to its full potential.

Correspondingly, the degree of emotional maturity and integrity in an organization will show up in the organization's actual core values. The **core values** provide the foundation that speaks to the noble essence of what the organization can be and should do to contribute to a better world.

Core values are an essential aspect that we too often quickly gloss over with nice-sounding platitudes. To the degree Steps I-III are in place, an organization can achieve greater depth of meaningful purpose, which includes but goes beyond increased profitability.

An in-depth study of an organization's core values offers an opportunity for individuals to look at what they want to spend a significant part of their life doing and being committed to. This is the base that provides a sense of meaningful commitment to something of perceived real value. This is the base that generates passion and creativity, opening opportunities previously not even considered.

The **strategic intent** is that impeccable focus and intention so compelling the vision can't do anything but manifest. Out of the strategic intent come the strategic objectives (usually a maximum of three, as more tends to disperse focus). **Strategic objectives** are the broad, key objectives that provide the framework for executing the organization's vision and values.

It is important to ensure that all strategic objectives are mutually reinforcing. If one is not obviously reinforcing the others, it is probably not a strategic objective. All subsequent plans, programs, projects, goals, and resource allocations must contribute to one or more of the strategic objectives or be eliminated. If they are not, they drain resources that could otherwise contribute to realizing the organization's vision. Without strategic objectives to benchmark against, there tends to be little or no coordinated focus, and resources thus tend to be dispersed, diluted, or otherwise wasted.

Operating principles are the boundaries of individual and organizational behavior that support the attainment of the strategic objectives and help ensure movement toward manifesting the vision. If we violate those boundaries of behavior, we expend resources on things that distract rather than support that movement. Operating principles need to be clearly defined, stated, understood, committed to, and honored. When imposed, rather than co-created, their workability, thus value, is limited. The vision, values, strategic intent, strategic objectives and operating principles must all be in alignment and mutually supportive. Co-creating these key elements is the fulcrum upon which the vitalization process rests.

Competing for the Future by Gary Hamel and C.K. Pradhalad offers excellent suggestions and insights to help facilitate this step. Another group of leading practitioners is The Institute of Cultural Affairs. The Institute's *Winning through Participation*, lays out methods to facilitate the co-creative process.

Co-creation brings focused intention into being and adds "juice" to the sense of teamwork and passionate commitment. In the absence of emotional maturity, co-creation and teamwork will not occur and the vision will remain little more than a flight of fancy, misdirecting potential and wasting resources.

Step V. Co-develop Strategic and Operational Plans

Out of a focused vision, core values, strategic intent and strategic objectives, people in an organization develop appropriate attention, focused intention, meaningful actions and a positive self-image. Without the cement of integrity, these can easily become inappropriate attention, dispersed intention, inadequate action, and a negative self-image. All programs, projects, goals and budgets should be co-developed to align with and support the strategic objectives. Duplicate the co-creative process, as appropriate, throughout the organization.

Another book by The Institute of Cultural Affairs, *The Art of Focused Conversation*, contains many participatory agendas for co-developing plans and addressing business issues.

Step VI. Implement Plans, Programs and Projects

Managing by the Numbers by Kremerr, Russuto and Case, is a common sense guide to financials and what they mean and is an excellent resource for making performance measures accessible.

Step VII. Reassess

Adjust, correct, and change the organization's plans, programs, projects and personnel as needed and appropriate. Continue to develop, reinforce and expand Steps I–III above, as needed.

Experience has shown, sometimes dramatically, that if foundational Steps I–III are conscientiously and competently developed, the resulting greater collaboration and teamwork not only increases efficiency and makes Steps IV-VII clearer and relatively effortless, but real productivity and morale skyrocket.

COMMON MISTAKES

It is important to lay a solid foundation. Far too often, Step V, planning, is attempted with little, if any, of the prior steps in place. Without the compelling vision and strategic objectives of Step IV in place, developing plans, goals and budgets does little more than tweak the existing system. Without a vision and aligned strategic objectives, management will, at best, devote resources primarily to planning and implementing improvements to the status quo. They may avoid ineffective fixes but, without a compelling vision, the emphasis will be much more myopic and will do little to truly invigorate the organization, deal with a changing competitive environment, foster innovation, or lead the organization in needed new directions.

Attempting to do Step IV, co-creating a compelling vision, without Step III, facilitating individuals to empower themselves, significantly reduces the chance of a truly compelling vision being created and manifested. Without Step III, the best one can hope for is willing compliance to someone else's vision rather than the much more expansive energy and motivation that is generated from a truly co-created vision.

Similarly, implementing any parts of Step III will have greater impact to the degree that Step II, educating the organization, is in process.

Step II simply will not happen to any meaningful degree without the intention and commitment of senior management, Step I.

A WORD OF CAUTION—THE IMPACT OF SELF-IMAGE

Self-image is a crucial part of change. What we are capable of achieving is limited by the actual image we have of ourselves. In fact, we will not obtain results that exceed our self-image. If, by fortuitous circumstances, results exceed that image, they cannot endure. Either they simply collapse, or the individual will sabotage those successes. What a person manifests will reflect his or her real self-image. The "size" of our self-image and thus the results and success we allow ourselves to manifest, directly correlates to our actual, not social, level of emotional maturity.

As the seven-step process recommended above is initiated, a synergy is created and a tremendous amount of energy, attention, intention, expectation and excitement is generated—the speed and magnitude of which can be astounding.

However, if the leader's actual self-image is smaller than the vision the group co-creates, that is a formula for disaster. A leader with a low self-image is a leader with a corresponding lack of emotional maturity, despite any public relations image or posturing to the contrary. That person will not allow the creation of an organization with a high level of emotional maturity. Conscious or unconscious, as irrational as it is, that person will regard an emotionally mature organization as a threat to his or her survival. As leader, he or she is in a position to and will sabotage the accomplishment of the vision until it contracts enough (or he or she gets removed) to be in alignment with his or her actual self-image. The leader will rationalize and justify every sabotaging act.

When we allow this to occur, we severely deflate hope, expectations and morale. Needed changes are not made, and opportunities are lost. In addition, the leader's successor will have an even more difficult time initiating any revitalization program, no matter how badly needed. Disillusionment or apathy concerning unfulfilled management initiatives is often the cause. People begin to think, "This too shall pass," and passive resistance to any management initiative becomes the norm. This is why honest assessment of Step I is crucial.

An individual's actual self-image (not the public relations façade) and what that person will manifest directly correlates with his or her actual integrity and emotional maturity. It therefore follows that **a person's integrity and emotional maturity should be among the Board of Director's top criteria in CEO selection and retention.**

POTENTIAL IMPACT

Adequately implementing and reinforcing steps I, II and III offers the greatest possibility for optimizing the selection, development and retention of an outstanding, emotionally mature leadership. It also encourages the growth of an organization in which all members feel they are learning and growing, are excited about the organization's future and their part in it, and view change as a welcome challenge and opportunity.

The degree to which these foundational steps are in place will be a primary factor in the ultimate success of the organization. Ultimate success means long-term viability and profitability in an environment of high morale and low turnover. It also means participating in an organization with a reputation for integrity, adaptability, innovation, excellence, outstanding customer service, and exceptional personnel development.

Points to consider:

- Can you find evidence of each step, I-VII, in your organization? If not, which steps are missing and what can you do to begin working on them?

LEADERSHIP FACTORS

Life has many nuances and subtleties. It is complex, and complexity is what allows and adds to life's richness and potential. Leadership, as a part of that complexity, has its own many interacting and interdependent aspects and factors, some of which are shown in the following chart (see Table 2.1). The emotionally wise leader will be strong in most, if not all, of the areas identified in the table. The arrows indicate the interactive aspects of the various factors and characteristics and the general directions in which those energies flow to manifest perceptions of reality. Integrity is shown as one of a number of interrelated factors. As will be pointed out in the next chapter, integrity is an individual and personal act of spontaneous responsibility. Importantly, integrity is also the wholeness of all these factors. They synergistically combine to be responsible presence, which is the essence of emotionally wise leadership.

THE DNA OF REAL LEADERSHIP

TABLE 2.1 - Leadership Factors

• **Presence** (being in the moment; facing the issues *now*) →	• **Courage** (willingness to confront one's fears, state an unpopular opinion)	• **Responsibility** (ability to respond—versus react—to whatever is present)	• **Integrity** (spontaneous responsibility; essence of emotional maturity) →
• **Self-respect** (honoring one's own emotions) →	• **Self-confidence** (knowing you can cope with whatever is)	• **Self-esteem** (one's self-evaluation)	• **Self-image** (perception of one's impact potential) →
• **Communication** (attention, intention, and duplication) →	• **Rapport** (affinity, respect for others)	• **Reality** (mutual agreement)	• **Understanding** (awareness and ability to apply it) →
• **Dialogue** (authentic two-way communication) →	• **Collaboration** (...with mutual concern)	• **Compassion** (...and caring)	• **Trust** (faith that one will deliver what is promised) →
• **Values** (consideration of importances) →	• **Principles** (behavioral boundaries that maintain values)	• **Vision** (ideal scene of a bigger, better future)	• **Vitality** (excitement and passion for expanded possibilities) →
• **Power** (ability and willingness to act) →	• **Character** (adherence to principle)	• **Empowerment** (giving one's self permission and authority to act)	• **Co-creative Action** (responsible alignment of imagination, desires and expectations) →
• **Intention** (impeccable focus, force and direction)	• **Determination** (strength of intention)	• **Perseverance** (persistence in overcoming resistance)	Impact Fulfillment Results Happiness Growth Joy

OPTIMIZING THE IMPACT OF TRAINING

Over the last several decades, thoughtful leaders have made significant progress in understanding organizational, managerial and leadership dynamics. Increasingly, senior management has been viewing practical implementation of these concepts and approaches as an investment rather than a cost.

Yet, for all the good ideas, the excitement, and the shift of awareness, few of the hot new concepts have manifested their hoped-for potential. Some were more difficult to apply than anticipated. Some turned out to have more fluff than substance. Some good ideas were simply oversold beyond their functional use or context. Some otherwise excellent concepts failed simply because of poor execution.

> *Barbara, an executive vice-president of a large national bank, said she would be sending over what she thought was a good management article. Barbara is a very competent manager of both people and tasks. She definitely is goal-oriented and does get results. She also does everything she can to encourage, develop, and "grow" her people not just functionally, but as human beings. She has been very proactive in this area and, in fact, has initiated numerous human-development programs for her staff. She brought in experts and hired consultants. She did all the "right things." Nevertheless, few of these programs have met with any real success. Her group did attain outstanding results, but more because of her leadership skills and sensitivities than because of the human-development programs. She spends a great deal of time personally coaching her people, doing what the programs have been unable to do. Overall, she is an enlightened and exceptional executive.*
>
> *Barbara said she strongly agreed with the article's emphasis, that management development should be focused, not on generalized human-development issues, but solely on the functional requirements of the business objectives. Of course, business*

objectives and the functional capabilities to achieve them are impor-
tant if not critical to an organization's survival and success. But why
would a competent, enlightened, caring individual who is honestly
concerned about the well-being and growth of her staff be in such
strong agreement with this exclusively functional focus? Her consis-
tently disappointing experience with developmental training programs
eventually convinced her that such programs did little, if anything, to
increase job performance. Unfortunately, that impression is often valid
for a number of reasons.

Following are some all-too-common reasons for mediocre, poor, or no results:

1. No program at all or a pretense of one;
2. Wrong focus—not addressing actual needs;
3. Poor design/poor execution;
4. Poor selection of participants;
5. Wrong sequence;
6. Inadequate follow-up support and reinforcement;
7. Missed synergies;
8. Inappropriate teaching methodology;
9. Limited scope.

Underlying all of these is a lack or only a superficial understanding of the dynamics involved in creating successful outcomes of developmental programs. However, many programs are well thought out by knowledgeable people who address real needs. Many are both competently designed and delivered. It is true that relatively few programs have adequate follow-up and reinforcement. It is also true that inadequacies in any one of the above could destroy the program's effectiveness. But, it is point number four where one of the biggest but least acknowledged problems lie—poor selection of participants.

Selecting Participants by Emotional Maturity

Emotionally mature people tend to be the most open, quickest, and most responsible students, and the most likely to creatively integrate and use their experience in a responsible, productive manner. Too often, however, there is little correlation between job function and emotional maturity. Unfortunately, management usually chooses participants by title and job function, not necessarily by emotional maturity.

The emotionally mature people who could really benefit from well-designed programs tend to be lumped with all the others. Most teaching is done to the lowest common denominator, so results will predictably be mediocre. No one wins, and the biggest losers are the organization and those mature individuals who could have really benefited except for the lowered standard of delivery to accommodate people who should never have been there in the first place.

Without competent evaluation of employees' emotional maturity, training programs are bound to fall short of expectations. What's left? Functional skills training specifically focused to attain particular business objectives. Certainly, business objectives need to be attained. Certainly, functional skills need to be developed to do so, but not as the **only or primary** consideration. **When maturity level is the senior and primary (not the only) consideration, management succeeds in developing the most responsible people, providing a sound, long-term organizational foundation. Because the participants are emotionally mature, they will be the most likely to responsibly learn or do what is necessary to provide the functional skills needed to meet the business objectives.**

The following elements, also key to training effectiveness, are likewise frequently ignored or given insufficient attention.

Doing the Right Things in the Most Effective Sequence

One rather significant reason why excellent concepts often do not fulfill their potential is that, in many cases, no one has provided the prerequisite foundation they need. For example, we tend to devote a tremendous amount of resources to needed functional skills development. However, unless underlying skills and attitudes, such as presence, listening, acknowledging, respecting the dignity of others, and the like are present, we will fail to optimize those resources.

We assume such foundational abilities are present, or we regard them as "too basic for our sophisticated people," or we simply ignore them. Unfortunately, a large percentage of the population actually lacks these basic skills. That shortfall can and does have a significant impact on overall training effectiveness and organizational performance.

Similarly, co-creating a vision and set of values is a critically important part of optimizing organizational and human capital. That co-creation can generate enormous aligned and focused energies. However, if we attempt such co-creation without first dealing with the repressed communication present among group members, we significantly reduce the possibility of the co-creation occurring. The same is true for any team-building program. Acknowledging and appropriately addressing these important prerequisites can contribute greatly to optimizing training effectiveness.

Developing Critical Mass

Critical mass is that state reached when the process becomes self-sustaining. Critical mass occurs when management provides sufficient reinforcement (following up with reinforcing programs) and sufficient volume (percent of target population trained) to reach a new norm.

Not uncommonly, excellent, well-designed, well-received programs delivered in the optimal sequence never reach their full potential simply because they were not sufficiently reinforced or delivered to enough people to accrue critical mass. When reinforcement of new desired behavior is lacking, individuals naturally tend to revert to the older, more familiar, and more comfortable behaviors. **Lack of sufficient reinforcement of good programs in sufficient volume is one of the most wasteful and costly mistakes continually made by management.**

However, when management provides sufficient reinforcement to enough people, critical mass is attained, and its self-reinforcing mechanism both greatly facilitates the desired behavioral change and exponentially expands training efficiency and cost-effectiveness. When management selects participants based on their emotional maturity, the numbers required to gain critical mass are significantly reduced, because those are the people who encourage and lead others to support responsible, needed programs.

Creating Elegant Synergies

Training courses are often little more than a series of stand-alone programs useful in themselves but not particularly complementary to anything else. Often, with only minimal extra effort or cost in design and implementation, fundamentals from other programs can be integrated and reinforced. This not only facilitates synergy but also movement toward critical mass.

Including People We Missed Before

Why do some people learn and others just don't get it? There is a significant minority of people who assimilate information and learn differently than is expected or taught in most educational institutions or programs. Thus, in the typical training course, these often very bright people are not exposed to needed information in a way that they can assimilate and use it. Such training is not helpful either to them or to the organization—both are deprived.

Recent research on how and why individuals think and assimilate (or reject) information differently has provided valuable new insights into the learning process. Only recently have people begun to understand and acknowledge some learning disabilities that were previously regarded as a source of embarrassment and denied or ignored. As *The Gift of Dyslexia* by Ronald Davis and Eldon Braun points out, some characteristics previously judged as dysfunctional can be a source of strength and unique ability when understood and supported. The same is true of Attention Deficit Disorder (ADD). Also understanding the various ways different personalities track and learn can be critical in optimizing the learning experience. An excellent resource is *The Enneagram Intelligences: Understanding Personality for Effective Teaching and Learning* by Janet Levine.

Incorporating various learning needs in training and program design and implementation makes a significant difference in increasing training effectiveness. It can expand significantly the number of people actually reached in the training process.

Fundamentals in Place

An organization will optimize its potential and use of resources to the degree the following are actually in place:

- Competent, committed, emotionally mature leadership;
- Appropriate foundational concepts and programs;
- Participant selection based on emotional maturity as a primary consideration;
- Competence in program design and delivery, including synergistic reinforcement;
- Programs and actions delivered in an optimal developmental and reinforcing sequence, including appropriate supportive activities, such as competent coaching and mentoring;
- Programs delivered in sufficient volume and concentration to attain critical mass.

3
Integrity—The Vital Factor

Attention, alertness, awareness, clarity, liveliness, vitality, are all manifestations of integrity, oneness with your true nature.
—Sri Nisargadatta Maharaj

Susan quietly slipped the stapler into her purse. "It really isn't stealing," she told herself. "The waste around here is unbelievable. They'll never miss it. Besides, Betty and Peter have practically equipped their entire home offices from here. And management, what do they do to deserve those big expense accounts? I deserve something, too!"

Meanwhile, twelve floors above, Eric was preparing for the Board meeting. Recently, a few members had been asking for more detail on the offshore projects. He reasoned, "Sure, the way the projects are set up a few of us will do well—and why shouldn't we?—the projects are all technically legal. But the Board is not operationally involved enough to fully comprehend the details. Too much information could be misunderstood. Better provide the minimum. No use creating unnecessary problems. Besides, the Board has never really understood, much less appreciated, what I've done for this company. Last year's bonus was a joke."

When we do something that we know isn't right, our automatic defensive reaction is to justify that action. We often project blame to distract ourselves, as well as others, from looking at our own irresponsible acts. These are not the behaviors of responsible, emotionally mature people. Not everyone is willing to look at how or why they exhibit those behaviors. However, for those who truly desire more integrity in their lives and are willing to look, what can they do?

To use an analogy, author and Nobel Peace Prize nominee Thich Nhat Hanh, when speaking of peace said, "There is no way to peace; peace, itself, is the way." In the same way, **there is no way to integrity, integrity itself is the way.** In other words, if we want more integrity in our life, we must act with more integrity.

How do we live and model integrity when few of us seem to understand or appreciate the real cost of its absence? Most of us can't state with precision what integrity is or differentiate it from morals, principles, or character. Integrity remains a somewhat nebulous ideal rather than a present and continual part of our life and behavior. Dictionaries provide little clarity; they tend to define related concepts in terms of each other. We need to take a deeper look at this elusive factor—what it actually is, its qualities, aspects, and impact. Then we may be in a better position to have integrity itself be the way.

As we consider the qualities and characteristics of integrity described in this chapter, we'll see that they are similar to and interdependent with the qualities and characteristics of emotionally wise leaders (described in the previous chapter) and also with those of emotional maturity (described in subsequent chapters). From that integrated perspective, we are better able to use those qualities and characteristics to become more emotionally mature and live wisely with integrity more of the time. Our competence in doing so depends largely on our clarity about and willingness to adhere to those things that are of fundamental importance to us as human beings—our values.

ESSENCE VALUES AND QUALITIES

Values (what we value) are qualities or symbols or things that we consider to be important. As there are levels of importance, there are levels of value. Some values are more fundamental than others, not "better" but more fundamental. The most fundamental values we refer to as "essence values."

Essence values are those energetic qualities that are core to our being. They are characterized by (1) inclusiveness rather than exclusiveness; (2) a presence that continually contributes to a more positive, loving environment; and (3) a stability independent of circumstance, context, social mores, or external sources of acceptance. Examples of essence values are the energies of love, allowance, empathy, authenticity, honesty, forgiveness, generosity and integrity.

Non-essence values do not consistently have the above three characteristics. Loyalty could be an example, for as highly regarded as it may be, it can be context-dependent, exclusive, and involve outside approval.

This is not to depreciate non-essence values. Books are written on the importance of values, such as the commitment and ability to execute and get results. Those values absolutely have their place and can inspire great contributions. However, we must keep them in perspective with their foundation and intention anchored in essence qualities. For example, the value placed on obtaining results must not have a priority greater then doing so with integrity. Essence qualities keep us in touch with our true power and ability to make real contributions. When this is forgotten, perspective is lost, priorities confused, decisions suboptimal or destructive and authority abused.

It's not hard to make decisions when you know what your values are.
—Roy Disney

WHAT IS HAVING INTEGRITY?

Dictionary definitions of integrity include: uprightness of character, honesty, the state or condition of being unimpaired, the state of being complete or undivided, nothing left out, whole, uncorrupted.

Key to understanding integrity is the concept of wholeness. Integrity is the inclusion and integration of the entirety of what is. That wholeness allows a presence to deal with whatever needs a response. It keeps us from being dispersed or feeling fragmented. It allows us to have impeccable focus when we so choose. That inclusive wholeness includes an awareness and appreciation of essence values. It allows the wisdom and the courage to make essence values our standard and their corresponding behaviors our priority. It allows the perspective and thus the confidence to know what doing the right thing is.

Whenever we act with integrity we immediately feel more expansive, more certain, more empowered. In fact, it is our integrity that is the foundation of and necessary quality to our personal empowerment. That wholeness gives our life depth, dimension, expanded choice and greater elegance and richness.

When any part is left out (for example, avoiding something) the integrity is broken—we disempower ourselves, and are thereby compelled to play the insatiable pretense game. Lack of integrity says, "I'm unable or unwilling (no power) to deal with some aspect (lack of wholeness) of what is and therefore, I am unable to fully respond (not response-able)."

Whenever we feel anxious, fearful, dispersed, or frustrated, we need to look at what we are avoiding. These are indications that our integrity is in jeopardy. When we sense we may not be able to deal with the entirety of what is occurring, we feel stress—a message that something needs to change.

If we ignore the message and the needed change does not occur, the stress builds and we are eventually overwhelmed, that is, we can no longer deal with the entirety of what is occurring. In other words, we loose integrity.

Trauma is the inability to integrate and deal with what is. Despite social pretenses to the contrary, lack of integrity is always traumatic and negatively affects all systems: physical, mental, emotional and spiritual.

Integration of all that **is** includes and embraces fear. As in quantum mechanics, observation itself literally transforms the object being observed. Its inclusion allows a synergistic use of its energy.

Think of integrity as a defining vibration with a very positive energy. When we add that vibration or frequency to any system, it necessarily creates a new, more positive resonance. When integrity is lacking, we lose the expansiveness and power of that synergy.

Looking at the anatomy of integrity, it is:

- Being present (presence, spontaneity);
- Responding to (responsibility);
- Whatever is (wholeness).

Having integrity is being responsibly able and willing (power) to face whatever needs confronting in the moment. **Integrity is the spontaneous assumption of responsibility or, simply, spontaneous responsibility.**

People of integrity take responsible action spontaneously. It is about responding—not reacting—now! It is about being responsible and accountable for our choices and actions—now!

As Senior Chief Jack Carlsen, United States Navy, likes to say, "Integrity is doing the 'right thing,' even when no one is looking." The action has to be spontaneous. If it is not spontaneous, the action is not one of integrity but of something else, influenced by what is deemed socially or politically acceptable. There are no shades of gray with integrity. We may generally be people of integrity, but on a particular subject at a particular time, we have it or we do not.

In summary, for a person to act with, have, or be of integrity, they must be willing and able to:

- Personally integrate essence values;
- Face whatever is present;
- Assess priorities based on essence values;
- Spontaneously act on those assessments.

INTEGRITY AND ITS IMPACT

Everything we do or don't do has impact. Whether we decide to work late, take a vacation, hire or fire an employee, buy a house, merge a company, or confront any difficult situation, each decision has an impact. In fact, because we don't live in a vacuum, everything we do has some impact on the larger world. The more positive the action, the more positive the impact. Conversely, the more negative our actions, the more negative our impact.

When we are willing and able to respond to whatever needs to be dealt with, we generate not just power (the ability and willingness to act) but, because of the synergy of that wholeness, we generate enormous power. Without integrity, we lose that synergy and its enormous potential.

Every time we compromise our integrity, we sacrifice a bit of our selves—we shave off a piece of the wholeness of who we are. The cost is huge: we become less present, less spontaneous, less able to respond, and therefore less powerful. We feel smaller and less confident. We are less willing to reach into the unknown. Innovation, or change of any kind, becomes increasingly threatening. We suffer, feeling dishonest, empty, separate, and alone as we play games in a plastic reality that increasingly seems to have little purpose.

Struggling to fill that void, we place increasingly higher demands on ourselves and project those demands onto others. The resulting performances and so-called successes, in whatever form, no matter how extraordinary, are never enough. We wind up feeling even more inadequate and unfulfilled, regardless of social, political, or financial achievements. Without that sense of wholeness, there is a chronic sense of separation, of alienation. Without integrity, we can never feel complete, truly content, satisfied, or happy with ourselves, our relationships, our environment, or with life.

People lacking integrity often try to compensate for this lack of power with false power. That is, they attempt to intimidate and manipulate in order to have "power over," which is always destructive no matter how justified.

Acting with integrity always has a positive, expansive, and constructive impact. Lack of integrity always has a negative, contracting, and destructive impact. Realize, however, that that impact, positive or negative, by contemporary social standards, may not be immediately obvious. Nevertheless, the impact is inevitable.

INTEGRITY IS PERSONAL

Integrity is not something anyone else can give to us or take from us. It has nothing to do with popularity or doing that which we deem politically or socially correct. When we have integrity, we spontaneously do the right thing based on values and principles that we consciously own—not on anything "imposed" from the outside. It's something you have to discover within yourself.

Integrity and morals are often confused. Morals are social codes of acceptable behavior within a particular group. What is considered moral and immoral can vary significantly among groups. These differences are often the basis of many "righteous" judgments.

Individuals can be very responsible and act with total integrity. But, if an individual's actions—even those of integrity—violate the codes of the group to which he or she belongs, that individual may be judged and labeled immoral by that group.

What is morality in any given time or place? It is what a majority then and there happen to like, and immorality is what they dislike.
—Alfred North Whitehead

Integrity is about you, personally, standing tall, acting on essence values and, sometimes, standing alone. In a world frequently lacking in integrity, acting with integrity can result in being ostracized.

Fear of being alone is a fundamental human fear. Real integrity is rare in a world full of insecure self-centered people doing things in order to be liked or accepted. Therefore, integrity demands and develops courage. Real courage is facing our fears and still acting responsibly.

Group conditions require an extra level of awareness. Sometimes individuals who have personal integrity go along with a situation because they assume someone else knows more about it than they and has the situation handled. When that is not the case, major problems can arise. Therefore, as General Chain stressed to his general staff, "It is vitally important for the integrity of the organization and its mission that we create and maintain an environment where concerns are freely expressed—where individuals are secure enough to say, 'I don't understand,' where assumptions are checked out, and where open dialogue is, in fact, the norm. It is only in such an environment that invalid assumptions are likely to be quickly spotted and corrected."

INTEGRITY IS A CHOICE

Integrity is a *conscious* choice—our conscious choice. Every situation we find ourselves in involves choice of some kind. Will we resist change? Will we withdraw from a confrontation? Will we celebrate a colleague's achievement, even though he or she may not celebrate ours? Will we ask the advice of a coworker, even if it means admitting we don't know the answer? Whether we actively participate in and contribute to a specific situation is our individual choice.

Even when confronted with difficult situations not of our own making, we can choose how to respond. We may try to convince the world and ourselves otherwise, but at some level, we recognize the truth: only we are responsible for our words and actions. Integrity is a conscious choice. Lack of integrity is also a conscious choice. Under all the excuses and denials, we know when we've violated our integrity. It is our choice and depends on nothing and no one except us.

Choices are made either reactively (fear-based and stagnating) or responsively (growth-generating). Insecure people are those who have not faced their fear, are thus stuck in fear and make fear-based choices. Those choices always lack integrity and are inevitably limiting no matter how justified.

Secure, mature people face their fear, listen to its message, integrate and positively utilize its energy. They are thus able to move beyond the fear and make integral, growth choices. People make growth choices only when they are willing and able to confront their fear.

When making any choice ask yourself, "Am I making this choice because I'm afraid to choose something else (avoiding choosing is a choice)? If it is fear-based, take several deep breaths and look again. You will find you are attempting to avoid confronting some self-perceived weakness and ignoring or discounting some strength. Before you commit to that fear-based choice—find the strength—and reevaluate that choice.

With integrity, we responsibly look at how we created, contributed to, or allowed a situation—positive or negative—to occur. We honestly own our part of it—no more, no less—and do what we can to improve a less-than-optimal situation without blame, self-pity, or regret.

At the same time, although we can model this quality and encourage others to take responsibility for themselves, we cannot take responsibility for others. Taking responsibility for another capable adult creates co-dependency, which manifests and prolongs a victim stance that always generates self-pity and resentment within both parties. When we live with integrity, we recognize that we are responsible for our own words and actions, and we respect the right of others to make different choices.

People with integrity have positive control over their lives and over the events in their lives. They have a clarity and certainty about what they want and will allow. They do not see life as happening **to** them, but rather, they make life happen.

When we are not true to ourselves, we are open to being controlled or manipulated by others. Without integrity, control (the ability to start, change or continue and to stop things under one's own determination) becomes a huge issue, and its distorted form becomes a compulsive need to manipulate people, things, or situations, either overtly or covertly.

True integrity is spontaneously choosing to act on our values and without hesitation, taking responsibility for the consequences of those choices. We do not live in a static universe. Either we choose to grow and become more of who we are, or we choose to contract and diminish our potential.

Every day, we choose between actions that lead to fulfillment and peace and those that lead to self-defeat and despair. The power of one choice can completely and instantaneously change our life.

Destiny is not a matter of chance; it's a matter of choice.
— William Jennings Bryan

INTEGRITY IS AT THE CORE OF WHO WE ARE

Integrity, or its lack, is the basis of the image we have of ourselves. We cannot create a sustainable reality that exceeds the fundamental image we have of ourselves. In other words, we make choices that naturally resonate with what we believe about ourselves. If we see ourselves as unimportant and incapable, it is impossible for us to make constructive, expansive decisions with any confidence. Alternately, if we have a healthy, positive sense of self, our decisions, actions, and results naturally reflect this self-image. When we try to make decisions that are at odds with our actual self-image, the outcome will usually be short-lived, reflecting this dissonance. We will unconsciously create or allow circumstances that force our reality to align with our core self-image.

If our goal or achievement is beyond our core self-image, we will sabotage it. This is a reason why so many people who have achieved great success end up destroying what they have built. It is also the reason why so many people who appear to be on the verge of success somehow muck it up. Despite all our bluster to the contrary, without integrity we cannot have a positive self-image.

INTEGRITY IS THE FOUNDATION OF VISION, PRINCIPLES AND CHARACTER

Integrity is the bedrock and the cement of our purpose, principles and character. It is the foundation that provides the willingness, ability, poise, presence, and certainty to deal with the *entirety* of what *is*. It is from this foundation that we develop our sense of value—what we value, how we value, and what our values are.

Out of that develops our sense of purpose and vision of what can be. In living our values and moving toward this ideal vision, we become more of who we truly are. Focusing on vision helps us see possibilities and enables us to plan with purpose and intention. Without the cement of integrity, we are left distracted, unclear about what to do, ineffective in action, and weighed down by negativity.

Our values, purpose and vision shape our principles. Principles, in this sense, are our self-chosen boundaries of behavior—of what we will and will not do in living our own values, maintaining our integrity, and moving toward our vision. They provide the framework for our actions.

In matters of style, swim with the current; in matters of principle, stand like a rock. —Thomas Jefferson

Our character is the degree to which we adhere to our principles. When we are clear about our values and principles, we can respond rather than react to any situation, including a hostile or manipulative one. We can play the game without being caught up in it. If we are not clear about our principles, we tend to react and feel controlled by external sources. We become a victim of the game rather than a causative, creative leader of the game.

Expediency is often used as a justification for violating or ignoring our principles. We may talk of ideals and principles, but if we are not true to them and do not act on them, no matter how much we talk about them, we are not individuals of principle or character. Consequently, we will not move forward in realizing our vision.

There is no substitute for integrity. Without integrity as our bedrock, we have no substantive sense of purpose, no noble vision, no clear principles of behavior, and no character. Without integrity, only pretenses of those exist. Without integrity, we feel a void of insufficiency and inadequacy. We attempt to fill it with substitute status symbols, like money, possessions, position and power. This hunger is insatiable. No matter how much we accrue, it will never be enough to fill that void.

Without integrity, episodes of frustration, confusion, denial and pretense increase. Integrity is the mortar that keeps our ideals, principles and character aligned and in place.

THE ESSENCE OF INTEGRITY

Integrity is integral to love, loving, and being loved. Love is about caring, responding to, and respecting ourselves and others with honesty and a depth of passion and compassion. Authentic love is the essence of integrity. Love without integrity manifests as shallow relationships and co-dependencies rife with dishonesty, deceit, invalidation, broken agreements, and generally abusive behavior. Without integrity, there is no real love, only superficial pretenses of it.

QUALITIES THAT DISTINGUISH PEOPLE OF INTEGRITY

Qualities that accompany integrity include presence, honesty, humility and discernment, to name a few. Let's explore some of these qualities in greater detail.

1. People of integrity exude presence. They are able to be attentive and in the moment rather than distant and distracted. They are willing to look at each moment afresh, without the filters of fixed ideas or preconceived notions. Integrity allows them to discern, evaluate, and reach conclusions relatively free of bias and prejudice. Without presence we cannot make responsible choices spontaneously. We cannot be spontaneous without being in the moment.

2. People of integrity are honest, authentic, and trustworthy. They are unafraid to look at themselves honestly. They recognize and own both their shortcomings and their strengths. The authenticity of their communication inspires confidence and trust. Authenticity is the basis of trust.

3. People of integrity act and live with dignity. As such, people of integrity truly respect others and themselves. They respect others while at the same time refusing to tolerate dysfunctional or hurtful behavior. Lack of respect for individual human dignity breeds indifference, intolerance, contempt, abuse and injustice. People lacking integrity not only have a lack of respect for others but also for themselves. Low self-worth, low self-esteem and the various manifestations of arrogance all lack dignity and indicate integrity's absence.

4. People of integrity have keen discernment. They regularly exercise the ability to distinguish and prioritize clearly without prejudice or bias. Because they exhibit presence, humility, honesty and respect for themselves and others, their ability to be discerning in any situation is optimized.

5. People of integrity have a wisdom that goes beyond mere knowledge. Wisdom is about being able to see and responsibly act on the big picture without losing sight of and being compassionate about the current situation. It is a presence with awareness. It includes but transcends logic and reason. From that awareness, people of integrity realize they are not isolated individuals but rather are part of a larger community, and that whatever they put out, positive or negative, will likewise, directly or indirectly, impact their life and those with whom they associate. Wise people are thus relatively free of the destructive patterns of greed and prejudice typical of those who are less aware. Consequently, they have a larger perspective and are able to provide insights that help bring the world more into balance.

6. People of integrity are compassionate. Compassion is more than kindness, it is awareness. People of integrity are sensitive to the needs, wants and desires both of themselves and others. Because they have the courage to face and responsibly address their own fears and suffering, they can recognize, understand and be compassionate about the suffering of others, while at the same time refraining from rewarding victimhood or creating dependencies, which would not be compassionate at all.

7. People of integrity are generous. They are secure enough that they don't have to hang onto things or viewpoints and so, they can easily share—thoughts, feelings, ideas and concerns, as well as material things. The willingness to share initiates a flow that not only tends to be reciprocated but also opens the sharer to innovation and change. That ability and willingness to share not only facilitates authentic communication but also creates a spaciousness that allows for even more—more relationships, more connection, more intimacy, more willingness to be, do, and have, more happiness, more peace, more caring, and more love. These, in turn, build more self-confidence, self-esteem and self-respect.

8. People who live with integrity experience dominion. Dominion is power and the ability to share that power with respect and honor. Its opposite is domination or power over others.

9. People of integrity are able to fully enjoy life. They are able to appreciate and enjoy what *is*–savoring the humor in life and appreciating its aesthetics and nuances. Having integrity means being able to be responsible without being dour–being able to spontaneously have fun. People of integrity have a passion for life.

Note that the qualities of people with integrity are also the characteristics of the emotionally wise leader noted in Chapter 2, page 33. In fact, one will not–and cannot–be emotionally mature or wise if integrity is lacking. **Our personal integrity defines the limits of what we allow ourselves to be.**

ASSESSING THE STRENGTH OF OUR INTEGRITY

How do we assess our integrity? We need to first look at what we are actually doing and assess whether it is responsible action that positively contributes to our perceived ideal. **The steps to getting there are the same as the qualities of being there.** If we want our environment to be a more responsible one, we need to be more responsible in the moment. If we want more love in our life, we need to be more loving. If we want to be heard more, we need to listen more. In other words, how are we at doing what we say we want?

To the degree we wait for someone else to do what we want done, we complain (overtly or covertly). What are your chronic complaints? Complaining is a symptom of a lack of integrity. Look where your complaints lie and confront how you've been passing the buck. You will find not one but two patterns that you follow virtually automatically. The first is how you pass the buck. The second is how you rationalize doing so.

Next, we need to assess our follow-through. Integrity means following through, with intention, on our stated or implied promises. It means not promising what we do not intend to follow up on or deliver. It means putting an end to excuses, rationalizations and justifications. It means choosing honesty over political expediency.

Points to consider:

- How often do you find yourself complaining?
- What is your most common, and repeating, complaint?
- Who or what do you most often blame?
- How frequently do you not keep promises and commitments?
- Can you spot your pattern of justification?
- What responsibility can you take in relieving or eliminating the sources of your complaints?

Let honor be as strong an obligation to us as necessity is to others.
—Pliny the Elder

WHEN INTEGRITY IS ABSENT: RECOGNIZING THE SIGNS

It is essential not to confuse the qualities of integrity with charisma, eloquence, charm, or even bottom-line performance. Those qualities and that performance may be very important, sometimes critical, but they are secondary to the fundamental importance of integrity.

Without integrity, other qualities or achievements will be corrupted and abused. When integrity is not a primary standard for all behaviors, is not highly valued for its own sake, or is considered impractical or unimportant or made into a joke or a non-issue, we can observe the following well-rationalized manifestations:

- Authenticity and candor are lacking and often criticized as unrealistic or naïve;
- Looking good becomes more important than being authentic;

- Showmanship and public relations gimmicks are substituted for leadership;
- Short-term performance increasingly becomes more important than long-term growth and sustainability;
- Ability to manipulate people, situations and stock prices is rewarded over creating honest communication, sincere relationships and substantive value;
- Competition becomes redefined as "beating the other guy," rather than a mechanism to bring forth our best;
- Respect for human dignity is ignored and shrinks to "taking care of me and only me";
- Vitality and productivity are replaced with pretense and busywork;
- Compromise degenerates into mediocrity rather than flourishing as a synergy of expanded viewpoints;
- Striving for excellence is replaced with insatiable demands for perfection;
- Vision and leadership wither to a focus on how to manage bureaucracy and issues;
- Compassion becomes "too expensive" or "not our business";
- Polls are used to pander for votes rather than to understand viewpoints and needs to communicate or educate;
- Loyalty becomes non-discerning agreement and support rather than forthright devil's advocacy;
- The letter of the law is used to subvert justice rather than to aid it.

Without integrity, our self-image and self-esteem become dependent on what other people think. When that happens, we inevitably feel inadequate. We expend enormous amounts of energy trying to compensate for that feeling of inadequacy but pretend otherwise. Decisions and actions become limited, mechanical, and trite. We wind up deceiving ourselves as well as others. Our self-confidence degenerates into arrogance or apathy, and our self-respect evaporates.

Without integrity, our character is replaced with political expedience. Concerns about money, power and status dominate and control our actions and life. We lose balance and perspective. Our compassion for and appreciation of the dignity of every human being deteriorates into insincere, self-centered, closed and unloving attitudes and behaviors. Without integrity, our dreams and vision lose their compelling energy. Our goals become mere mechanical objectives without "juice." Our passion for life disintegrates into a compulsive, anxiety-ridden, insatiable need for success or simply deteriorates and dies.

As we view contemporary society, how often do we observe examples of jealousy, envy and greed accompanied by pretense, denial, and dishonesty? These are the dysfunctional compensations for underlying feelings of insecurity and powerlessness. Alcohol, drugs and overwork are often used to numb those feelings. We see how lack of integrity precludes authenticity and thus destroys credibility and trust and devastates relationships and security.

We notice that many of our contemporaries are chronically angry, confused, afraid, defensive, depressed, despairing, apathetic, shallow, work-obsessed, burned out, or wanting to drop out. We see too many who are "leading lives of quiet desperation" and not consciously having the slightest idea of how to do anything about it. In fact, what we are noticing are all symptoms of a lack of integrity. Without integrity, we are unhappy and far, far less than we could be.

When integrity ceases to be a primary standard, the true costs are beyond measure. Developing social skills and bottom-line abilities can be an important adjunct to, but never a replacement for, acting with integrity.

A resource on integrity and values is *Accountability* by Rob Lebow, the originator of the *Values Tension Index* used to measure cultural resilience in organizations.

FUEL FOR POWERFUL CHANGE

Whenever we feel powerless, we need to find where we have violated our sense of personal integrity and correct it. If we feel "caught in the game," or that "there is nothing we can do about it," or we "have to stoop to their level to survive," we must realize that all of those feelings are additional symptoms and messages indicating a lack of integrity. In this condition, our ability to view other possibilities is severely restricted. We feel powerless.

Correspondingly, we will blame, deny, lie, manipulate, feel self-pity, and act victimized. Instead of being responsible, we will be irresponsible. We will justify, rationalize, or attempt to explain away even our most blatant irresponsibilities and self-imposed limitations.

People with integrity have a clear, unshakable presence. They have determination and do what responsibly needs being done. They do not succumb to playing manipulative games because "that's the game out there." They do not whine, justify, or say they had no other choice. If they leave a position, they do so because they choose to, not because of anger, frustration, fear, grief, or apathy, but because of a preference based on recognition of what is responsible. They have a sense of certainty and self-confidence. They can—and often do—have strong opinions and are willing to express them when it is helpful to do so. They have a certainty and self-confidence that is neither self-righteous nor arrogant. Self-righteousness and arrogance, like false power, are compensations borne of fear, and they are always used to make ourselves right and others wrong.

When we act with integrity, the resulting level of poised certainty transcends any and all current consensus games and standards. Thus, by its very presence, integrity, even without any apparent action itself is power and creates positive change.

Gandhi's integrity, for example, so empowered him that he had far greater impact than any of the powerful politicians of his time. That influence even transcended the hatred of vastly different cultural and religious persuasions. Likewise, leaders are poised to have far greater impact on others and their organization when they are motivated by and act out of integrity. Integrity provides powerful fuel for appropriate and responsible change.

Hold yourself responsible for a higher standard than anyone expects of you. Never excuse yourself. —Henry Ward Beecher

PUTTING INTEGRITY INTO PRACTICE

To regain our integrity or really change anything, we first must be willing to honestly face and recognize when we are not living with integrity. This can be hard to look at. We may struggle with self-pity. We may be inclined to blame others. Blame is a way of projecting our own denials. Blame precludes real assessment of responsibility. It closes the door on constructive decisions and actions.

1. The first step is to recognize when integrity is missing. Where in our life are we fearful, anxious, angry or blaming? Where do we feel out of balance? These feelings are indicators of some struggle with doing the right thing and acting with integrity. Continuing upsets and problems are messages that there is still something(s) sticking around for which we haven't yet been willing to recognize and take responsibility.

Acknowledgement of what has happened is the first step to overcoming the consequences of any misfortune. —William James

2. Secondly, we need to own that we, and only we, are responsible for our choices, decisions, and actions. We need to own fully our part (no matter how big or small) of how we created, allowed or contributed to the condition (problem, upset) in which we find ourselves.

You have got to do your own growing, no matter how tall your Grandfather was. —Irish proverb

3. Thirdly, we need to either (a) honestly acknowledge and honor our accomplishments, or (b) forgive ourselves for having messed up. Maybe we could have done something better, more elegantly, more lovingly, more honestly, or with more courage, but we did not. Wallowing in self-pity and regret never does anything except keep us stuck in the muck. We need to let the recriminations go and realize we did the best we could with the awareness and resources we had at the time. We need to drop the self-pity, make the appropriate amends as we honestly can, and forgive ourselves.

On the other side of the coin, most of us could also do a better job at acknowledging ourselves when we do contribute. If we do not either appropriately acknowledge or forgive ourselves, we will not move on to the last step.

Self-pity is our worst enemy, and if we yield to it we never do anything wise in the world. —Helen Keller

4. We need to do something truly different. Real change means learning from our mistakes and doing something different. Such change may be difficult if not impossible to see now, but if we honestly and thoughtfully work through the first three steps, then we will know what to do to bring about true change with integrity.

No longer talk about the kind of man that a good man ought to be, but be such. —Marcus Aurelius

INTEGRITY AND EMOTIONAL MATURITY

Acting with integrity is both a vehicle for developing our maturity and the very expression of that maturity. If we are honestly willing to confront our confusion, doubt, and fear, and if we are willing to take action, make mistakes, and view those mistakes as learning opportunities, then progress is not only possible but assured. In this sense, practice does make perfect. Once we recognize and own that we alone are responsible for our choices, forgive ourselves for our mistakes, and start acting responsibly, then we can assume the mantle of true maturity. We'll explore more about emotional maturity in Chapter 5.

INTEGRITY AND THE GAMES OF LIFE

1. Life consists of games.
2. The anatomy of a game is a barrier to be overcome, with the outcome unpredictable.
3. If the outcome is predictable, it is not a game.
4. Games provide the challenges that test and strengthen our purpose and give us a sense of accomplishment.
5. We all need games—everyone plays them.
6. The anatomy of a problem is similar to the anatomy of a game. The difference is that a problem includes some denial of responsibility. That's what makes it a problem.
7. Responsibility is the ability to appropriately and constructively respond (versus react) to what is.
8. If we think playing the game (or having the problem) is up to someone else, we are playing the role of victim.
9. There are no victims, only volunteers.
10. When we are lacking in games, we will create problems in their stead (if we are being irresponsible and blaming) and act like a victim.
11. No one can solve anyone else's problem.

12. If we try to solve someone else's problem, the person will resist our solution and resent us.

13. There are all kinds and sizes of games (and problems).

14. Growth is about shifting from old games to bigger and more productive games.

15. Each game has its own rules.

16. If we want to play a game, we need to learn (or create) the rules of that game.

17. Wanting the benefits of the game without a willingness to play by its rules is arrogant, alienating, frustrating to all parties, and always unproductive.

18. If we don't like the rules or the game, we need to responsibly change them, or find or create another game.

19. We and no one else chooses whether we play.

20. Not making a choice is a choice.

21. Control is the ability to start, change or continue, and stop or complete the game (or problem) under one's own determination.

22. Power is both the ability and the willingness to act.

23. We can't be truly powerful without being responsible.

24. Integrity is the spontaneous assumption of responsibility.

25. Without integrity, we have neither control nor power and, as compensation, will attempt to have "control over" and "power over" others, overtly or covertly, or be "the victim" of someone else's games.

26. Games lacking integrity are always destructive—there are no exceptions.

27. Integrity trumps contemporary social mores and political considerations.

28. Sometimes, acts of integrity are interpreted as a threat to current values and vested interests. Consequently, they may be subject to rejection or attack.

29. An integral part of integrity is courage—the willingness to face one's fears and still act responsibly.
30. At any moment, we have integrity or we do not. There is no middle ground.
31. The measure of our integrity is **the** measure of who and what we are.
32. With integrity, we are whole. Without integrity, we are significantly less than we can be.
33. There is nothing more important than our integrity.

Thus, we may want to consider:

- What games are we playing?
- How are they really contributing beyond ego gratification?
- Are they hurting anyone?
- How do we rationalize that hurt?
- What games do we truly want to play?
- What games don't we want to play?
- What games are we willing to start, change, continue or stop and do so with integrity, courage and intention?

Tomorrow is always tomorrow. To put power back into our lives, we need to start **now**!

When the one great scorer comes to write your name, he marks not that you won or lost, but how you played the game. —Grantland Rice

SUMMARY
INTEGRITY—THE KEY TO A FULFILLED LIFE AND THE LINCHPIN TO DYNAMIC LEADERSHIP

Integrity is the spontaneous, conscious assumption of personal responsibility. It is the willingness to include the wholeness of what is that gives us depth and breadth. It provides us with a sense of substance. It is a frequency of energy that creates a positive, transforming resonance. Integrity is sensitive to, but transcends, moral codes and considerations of limitations. It precludes blame, regret, denial and self-pity. It creates and demands in us an appreciation of and passion for human dignity. Integrity is the basis of our dignity, grace, and sense of personal value and self-esteem. It manifests profound presence. It assures our honesty, our authenticity, and our trustworthiness.

Integrity puts us in touch with our true power and our unlimited potential. It gives us an awareness of possibilities that would otherwise seem unfathomable. It generates our ideals and principles and produces our character. It provides calm, certainty, self-confidence; courage to face our confusion, doubt and fear; and willingness to do what is right. Integrity is what focuses and develops our attention, intention, actions, and a self-image that aligns with and supports our ideals and principles. It allows us to enjoy love and happiness. Integrity gives meaning to life.

Without integrity, we are not whole. With it, we are responsible, loving, caring, creative, courageous, and empowered. There is nothing more important than our integrity. Our integrity is our bottom-line. **Integrity is more than an important factor. Integrity is the *vital* factor!**

The remainder of this book is dedicated to clarifying how we can proactively facilitate a culture and environment of integrity.

THE DNA OF EMPOWERMENT

4
Emotional Intelligence and Beyond

He who has so little knowledge of human nature as to seek happiness by changing anything other than his own disposition will waste his life in fruitless efforts and multiply the grief he intends to remove. —Samuel Johnson

MOVING TOWARD GREATER INTEGRITY

At any particular time, either we have integrity or we do not. Therefore, from a developmental perspective, questions arise as to its facilitation. As mentioned in the Introduction, the key is to recognize the relationship of integrity and emotional maturity. Integrity is the core of emotional maturity. If an individual is emotionally mature, that individual acts with integrity. The reciprocal is also true. If a person lacks integrity, we also know that person is not emotionally mature, despite any pretenses or protests to the contrary. Because of this correspondence, increased emotional maturity equals increased integrity.

Fortunately, emotional maturity is something we can look at in stages of development. If we can facilitate emotional maturity, we have a means to facilitate indirectly increased integrity.

Before we do so, we will first look at emotions themselves. This chapter is intended as an emotional intelligence primer to help us better understand the emotional dynamics involved in moving toward emotional maturity.

If we want to effectively communicate with, relate to, persuade, lead, and motivate others, it is a gross understatement to say it is helpful to understand what makes people tick. It's not simply helpful—it's crucial. And to understand others, we need first to understand ourselves. We need to know more about the dynamics that motivate our behaviors and intentions. We need to understand what influences our perception of ourselves, of others, and of the world.

Until we become more aware of how human emotional dynamics function, we tend to flounder in a world of uncertainty and insecurity—not a great foundation for leadership or anything else. We need to grow in emotional intelligence.

If a person is to get the meaning of life he must learn to like the facts about himself—ugly as they may seem to his sentimental vanity—before he can learn the truth behind the facts. And the truth is never ugly.
—Eugene O'Neill

EMOTIONAL INTELLIGENCE

You may have heard the statement, "Emotional intelligence is the ability to manage your emotions." Sounds reasonable, but what exactly does that mean? How do we go about managing our emotions? Some may say, "Hey, I do that all the time," meaning "I just stuff the uncomfortable or socially unacceptable emotions." Unfortunately, that's how many people "manage" their emotions. Rather than repressing them, we need to become more effective in using our emotions to more constructively deal with the ups and downs of life.

People's responsiveness to new ideas, their flexibility to change, and their willingness to support a plan or action varies with their emotional state. How people **respond** or **react** to any situation varies with their emotional state. For example, people who are angry perceive life and how they need to go through it differently than people who are cheerful or people who are grieving. Each person's interpretation of the same circumstance as well as their priorities will vary depending on their emotional state. Correspondingly, the type of communication that will be meaningful and effective will vary with the individual's emotional state. When we are reactive rather than responsive, emotions seem to run our lives and we are at a loss about what to do.

In order to address adequately the influence of emotions in our lives, we need to take a closer look at what constitutes emotional intelligence. Emotional intelligence is having an awareness of the following:

1. What emotions are;
2. Their purpose, meaning, and what they can tell us (if we listen);
3. The different behaviors and attitudes associated with each emotion;
4. The relationship among emotions;
5. How we tend to misuse emotions;
6. How to use emotions to more effectively relate and communicate.

In part, emotional intelligence is gaining clarity about how we have been intimidated, controlled and limited and, importantly, how we allowed that to happen. We did so by blindly adhering to our fear-based negative ego patterns. As we recognize and assume ownership of those self-generated and self-sustaining patterns, we begin to have greater choice in either working with them or letting them go. Making an increasing number of conscious choices about our patterns of behavior is a positive sign that we're becoming more responsible, that is, maturing and owning more of our inherent power.

WHAT ARE EMOTIONS?

Emotions (energy in motion) are messages from our subconscious that are intended to enhance our survival choices and actions by providing us with environmental information. They act as filters through which we interpret life by directing us to where we need to focus our attention to optimize our survival potential.

Each discrete emotion conveys a specific message that indicates the relative degree of security or potential threat perceived to be present. Where anyone is emotionally in this hierarchy, indicates how much stress they are under. Thus, emotions have a specific order and relationship to one another, a hierarchy. Different predictable behaviors, attitudes and forms of communication correlate with each of the various levels of stress or security. Importantly, where a person is emotionally on this scale also indicates the potential of that person for creating positive change.

Understanding this hierarchy can be extremely helpful in assessing a person's emotional maturity and, correspondingly, his ability to contribute positively to himself, to others, and to an organization.

It is important to recognize that emotions are not inherently good or bad, positive or negative. They are simply messages. Issues can arise when we make judgments that some emotions are "better" than others are. We usually do that because we are more comfortable with the "nice" emotions, such as cheerfulness and enthusiasm. We tend to label those emotions as "good" and the others, such as anger, fear and grief, as "bad." Assignments of "good" and "bad" are value judgments. They are opinions, not facts. When we ignore, avoid, deny, or repress the emotions we do not like, we lose access to their messages. This limits our decisions, choices and actions.

Emotions become a problem when we ignore them. Too often, because of an unwillingness to be present with a particular feeling, we choose to avoid the messages of our emotions. Repressing the messages of emotions creates a negative, destructive result.

To **repress** an emotion is to know we have it but not express it. To **suppress** an emotion is to pretend to ourselves we don't have it when we do. To **harbor** an emotion is to have and express it repeatedly but never let it go.

Various emotions give us a means to discern subtleties and nuances, providing greater depth and richness to our perceptions and experiences. The more access we have to our emotions, the greater our ability to discern more of the richness and subtleties of life. When we ignore or repress our emotions, we lose that ability and gift.

Repressing any emotion represses the feedback it could provide and, thus, limits our communication with ourselves as well as with others. When we do not listen to our emotional messages, we miss information that would otherwise contribute to our ability to adapt, survive, innovate, create, and enjoy life.

When we ignore the emotional message because it is not to our liking, the emotion does not just go away. It accumulates and becomes louder. The repressed emotion eventually turns into a "shout," but too often, we still do not listen, because at that stage it is not only inconvenient, but also uncomfortable. When the shout turns into a "scream" of crisis, we usually react rather than respond.

This accumulative process of avoiding the uncomfortable and unfamiliar is why much of all needed change, by individuals and organizations, builds to crisis and, far too often, takes a tragedy before we institute needed reforms.

People also often repress "nice" emotions and their accompanying messages, with the same limiting result. Someone who is feeling enthusiasm but represses it because of a hostile environment is being as inhibited and reactive as one who represses anger or grief. For example, Joe is enthusiastic about being hired to work on what he considers an exciting project. However, the organization he joined places a very high value on being "professional," which it interprets as "proper and serious." Excitement and enthusiasm are regarded as frivolous and childish and are therefore frowned upon as being unprofessional. So rather than risk being considered "inappropriate," Joe plays it cool and acts appropriately serious—and with those accommodations, his enthusiasm and excitement evaporate. Joe moves from being a motivated producer to being a mediocre performer. Such behavior may be socially or politically correct, but the emotional and behavioral consequences are always limiting.

Additionally, it is faulty reasoning to assume we can stifle any one emotion without affecting others. When we repress any emotion, we also repress our ability to access, feel, use and appropriately express our entire span of emotions. For instance, we cannot stifle our anger or fear without also stifling our enthusiasm and joy. This is one of the reasons why many people seem to have a limited emotional range or appear mono-emotional, that is, always angry, sad, despairing, or even cheerful (which is a cover). The lack of emotion appropriate to a circumstance is as much an indication of heavy repression as is an explosive, out-of-proportion reaction.

Permitting ourselves to feel fully each emotion as it occurs provides us with greater information, increasing our ability to take optimum appropriate action. As we allow ourselves to feel more of our emotions, we become more present. We gain more timely information and greater sophistication in differentiating the nuances of the messages, enabling us to respond quickly, precisely, and appropriately.

By feeling more of our emotions we access more of our inherent talents and strengths. That willingness and ability correspond directly to our potential effectiveness in all areas of interpersonal interaction. The more we are in touch with our emotions, the greater our ability to differentiate and add subtlety, nuance, depth, and richness to our perceptions. Therefore, access to all of our emotions and their messages is a necessary ingredient to our overall emotional intelligence.

Cherish your own emotions and never undervalue them. —Robert Henri

DIFFERENTIATING AUTHENTIC FROM ARTIFICIAL EMOTIONS

Authentic, or real, emotions have both positive and negative potential. Anger, fear, and grief are examples of authentic emotions, in that they have positive as well as negative potential.

Emotionally mature individuals appropriately feel anger in the face of irresponsibility, injustice, or manipulative behavior. The anger is their message that some responsible action needs to be taken. They convert the anger into an energy that will have a positive, corrective effect.

Fear can paralyze, but it can also focus a person's attention in the **now**, generating the adrenaline needed for quick action and surviving an attack. Grief can help to develop sensitivity and compassion. If an emotion does not have both positive as well as negative potential, it is not an authentic emotion, but an artificial emotion.

Humankind creates artificial emotions as an attempt to avoid dealing with the real underlying emotions—most often anger, fear, shame, or hurt. Unlike authentic emotions, artificial emotions have no redeeming qualities or aspects, only negative ones.

When someone employs an artificial emotion, realize that that person is feeling overwhelmed to some degree and is attempting to avoid dealing with what is really going on. Guilt, martyrdom and victimhood are examples of artificial emotional states.

Guilt

Guilt is an artificial emotion used to suppress and deny our anger, fear, shame, or hurt. It is a mechanism to pretend we are attempting to take some semblance of responsibility when we are not. It is an attempt to gain some form of manipulative control to compensate for a sense of being out of control. It has no positive aspects or potential. We use guilt to misdirect our repressed underlying emotion and to beat up on ourselves and others rather than feel the depth of our caring and love for someone or the sadness of an opportunity lost.

A person using guilt to distract and avoid responsibility may say things like, "I obviously feel guilty. Isn't that enough? You should feel sorry for me because I feel so guilty." Another example of using guilt to manipulate is some statement to the effect of, "After all I did for you, and you can't do this for me?"

Guilt is not the same as remorse. Remorse is a real emotion of feeling truly sorry for the hurt we caused or allowed but which cannot be corrected. Remorse needs to be felt—fully. Only when fully allowed, owned, and felt can it resolve the depth of our pain. Its positive potential, similar to that of grief, is the expansion of our sensitivity, compassion, and empathy. Fully felt remorse helps to cultivate an increased awareness of sensitivity to, and responsibility for how our actions impact life. Guilt, however, has no redeeming aspect or potential.

Indulging in guilt is always destructive. Allowing remorse is liberating. If you feel caught in guilt, ask yourself, "What emotion—anger, hurt, fear or shame—am I attempting to cover by using guilt?"

Martyrdom

Martyrdom is an emotional state characterized by attitudes and feelings of being:

- Unappreciated;
- Misunderstood;
- Hopeless;
- Burdened with impossible demands;
- Innocent of all wrongdoing;
- Mistreated and misjudged.

Martyrs seldom directly express their anger, fear, shame or hurt or the reasons for it. Instead, they exhibit the following behavioral patterns:

- Self-righteousness;
- Refusal to acknowledge any wrongdoing;

- Inability to feel or accept gratitude;
- Quietly seek revenge;
- Lie;
- Expect noble exoneration in the future.

Martyrs create circumstances that will justify their feelings of being unappreciated and misunderstood. The energy of a martyr is based in un-confronted fear and is always hostile. Despite the denials, pretenses, and often sophisticated façades, the behavior of a martyr is vicious and destructive.

Victimhood

Victims have the same characteristics as martyrs, only their expression is less sophisticated. The difference is victims, unlike martyrs, are overt and expressive of their anger, hurt, fear or shame and why they feel that way. Behavior common to victims is that they want others to do things for them because of their "sad" condition but are never satisfied with whatever is done.

Both victim and martyr roles are subtle combinations of self-pity and self-importance. Alone, those characteristics are more obvious. Combined, the self-pity and self-importance cover each other and are much harder to spot and more destructive.

As long as we feel victimized, we give up our power to change.
—Anonymous

FEAR AND ANXIETY

Fear and anxiety are authentic emotions, with both positive and negative potential. Both provide messages to us without which we could be vulnerable. However, fear and anxiety are different, and it is important to distinguish between the two.

Fear

Fear is the automatic response to anything that is different from what was. It is about the threat of potential future loss (real or imagined) and is related to a specific incident or event.

Benefits of fear

- Fear is a whisper (a warning) that tells us to watch out, that there may be some threat present. It is like a smoke alarm.
- Fear tells us where there is a lack of trust in a person or situation.
- Fear can slow us down enough to provide the opportunity to change directions.
- Fear tells us we have a belief that is contra-survival and directs us as to where we need to be more responsible.

Liabilities of fear

- Fear can lead to our feeling that we are no longer in control. We can allow it to disempower us by our avoidance of or exaggerated reaction to it.
- Fear can paralyze us so we cannot make choices. Fear always accompanies change and, therefore, acts to prevent it. A little bit of fear gives us pause, too much fear paralyzes us.
- Fear keeps the past alive in the present. Fear of repeating errors of the past can prevent us from accurately assessing the present.
- Fear can be addictive. It is easy to get caught in it, and it is self-replicating.
- Fear becomes the rationalization for the manipulations of power playing: "If I am not on top that means someone is on top of me. Therefore, whatever I do to get on top is justified."

Many people use fear in their attempts to control, manipulate, intimidate, and dominate others. Their behavior is a projection of their own insecurities and is inevitably hurtful and destructive.

A major key to personal growth and emotional maturity is dealing with how to face fear. Courage is not the absence of fear. Rather, it is the willingness to face our fear, listen to its message, act accordingly, and move beyond it. When we fail to face our fear, authenticity, sincerity and honesty disappear, and effective communication becomes impossible.

Any time we notice people, including ourselves, lacking in those qualities, we can assume they have fears they are not confronting. All limiting behaviors come out of some form of an unwillingness to face our fears. When that happens, we become paralyzed and thus controlled by our fear, and we do not take appropriate action.

When we do not face our fears, we experience a sense of being out of control. Thus, issues concerning control—whether we feel "always controlled," "never in control," "must be in control," or "won't be controlled"—wind up dominating our life. We develop compensating skills to make us feel we are in control.

Our compensating, compulsive actions can cover a considerable range of behaviors, exemplified by the overcautious naysayer, the domineering tyrant, the workaholic overachiever, the fun-only rationalizer, the withdrawn intellectual, the entitled snob, the passive-aggressive procrastinator, the "helpful" martyr, and the guilt-producing victim. All of these roles are attempts to regain some form of control, to be "safe." All are insatiable and destructive.

The way out is the way through. The real treasures lie on the other side of our fear. When we truly confront our fears, we see things we did not see before. It is that clarity that seemingly miraculously transmutes the fearful or anxious energy into constructive survival action. When integrated, fear transmutes to sensitivity, aliveness and excitement. As we confront our fear, listen to its message and take responsible action, limitations begin to dissolve and our entire universe expands.

You gain strength, courage and confidence by every experience in which you really stop to look fear in the face. —Eleanor Roosevelt

Anxiety

Anxiety is different from fear in that it is not associated with a specific event or a specific time. Anxiety is free-floating and usually results from one or more of the following general characteristics:

- Undefined pain, anger, hurt, or fear;
- Expectation of error, e.g., "I will be less than perfect";
- Anticipated rejection or humiliation;
- Disbelief in a positive future;
- Trust erroneously placed in a situation, another person, or ourselves if we are untrustworthy.

Anxiety is more insidious than fear because it is harder to define. Neither fear nor anxiety can be handled without being defined. The first step in dealing with either is to get as focused and as specific as possible in determining exactly what we are fearful of or anxious about.

Often asking repetitively, "And what's under that?" will help get us closer to the specifics of the cause of our anxiety. That clarity itself helps dissipate the anxiety.

Nothing in life is more remarkable than the unnecessary anxiety which we endure, and generally create ourselves. —Benjamin Disraeli

ARROGANCE

No one would describe Robert as arrogant. He was professional, well-mannered, and gracious. In handling the sale of his company, he felt confident that he had handled the negotiation very well. Just like an experienced negotiator should, he had set high, but not ridiculous, goals and stuck to them. He had established good rapport, determined the other party's needs, met them, and positioned himself well. They, not he, had made the first offer, and he had conceded slowly in small amounts.

Finally, with only a few details left to handle, he was about to close the deal. Then he made his fatal mistake: the other side was making some comments and, feeling the deal was in the bag, Robert only listened casually. They noticed his detachment. In that instant they felt discounted and lost trust in the sincerity of his claims. His casual inattention was a form of "subtle arrogance," and it cost him a multimillion-dollar deal.

Defining Subtle Arrogance

Arrogance is sometimes obvious to the onlooker. No one likes the know-it-all who flaunts his or her self-importance. We often condemn such a person. However, subtle arrogance comes in many forms and can be just as much if not more dangerous.

Consider the following situations:

- An interviewer takes several phone calls during your interview;
- Someone interrupts you to make his point;
- Your boss ignores your input;
- Someone only pretends to listen to you.

In each situation the person is effectively communicating, "I and my needs are more important than you and your needs."

These behaviors, which we all occasionally exhibit, are subtle forms of arrogance. Subtle or blatant, arrogance of any form is always destructive to any relationship, regardless of the circumstances and no matter how justified. If you lack presence and display any form of inattention or disinterest, you run the risk of making the other person feel discounted, which immediately breaks rapport. As Robert discovered, it doesn't take blatant arrogance to destroy a negotiation—subtle arrogance does just as much damage.

The Root of Arrogance

The basis of arrogance, subtle or not, lies in our own insecurities. Basically, we are all striving for growth, expansion and awareness. Unfortunately, "striving to be better" is sometimes twisted into demands by parents and society to be "better than." In constantly needing to be better than others, we are under pressure to repress our fear, insecurity, hurt, and anger. The result is often a façade of being "better than." Acting "better than" is a cover for an underlying insecurity, that is, some sense or feeling of being "less than."

That façade is the face of arrogance. When we exhibit it, it keeps us distant from others. It "protects" us from looking at our fears. The more fearful we are the more we must defend and maintain that façade at all costs. To do this we must, to some extent, blind ourselves to other viewpoints and put boundaries around our own.

The result is always limiting. It limits our ability to listen, observe, evaluate, adapt and change. It limits our ability to maintain rapport, learn and expand.

We're human and, as such, we're not perfect. On occasion, we all can be arrogant. If we truly want to be more effective, we must limit not only the destructive impact of that arrogance, but also the arrogance itself. Fortunately, if we want to, we can choose to correct arrogant behavior.

As a start, we must have an honest willingness to examine our behavior and look at what is causing the arrogance. What is the underlying fear that the façade covers? This can be a tough question to answer. But if we confront this fear honestly, the effects can be amazing.

The steps to handling arrogance are as follows:

1. Sincerely admit, "Sometimes I am arrogant."
2. Look for the specific ways you discount or belittle other people. Ask yourself things like, "When and how was I insensitive? When and how did I interrupt? When and how did I act "better than"? These acts of arrogance are often

preceded by feelings of envy, resentment, or boredom. Never allow small episodes of arrogance to slip by because of their "size." Any time we discount another person, it is a put-down. And a put-down is never a small thing! Far too often, it has huge consequences—and they are always negative.

3. Look for a pattern of the ways in which you discount other people.

4. Look at how you rationalize each act of discounting. Find your pattern of excuses and justifications. Under the pattern, own what you are avoiding.

5. Face that fear by choosing to confront and fully feel it. Feel the fear in your body. Stay with it and simply observe what comes up until it dissolves. Feel the expansiveness and sense of freedom doing so provides.

6. Acknowledge yourself for your courage and determination. Celebrate!

7. Take appropriate corrective action, which will now be obvious and relatively effortless. Celebrate again!

If we do this whenever we are having difficulties or are upset with others, we will soon find both our arrogance and people problems significantly lessen.

When we do not confront our fears, we are making ourselves susceptible to manipulation. Others who discover our fears can use them against us to gain control of our actions. For example, during negotiations, people may use manipulative tactics to get the other person to concede. How? They find and focus on the person's fears and insecurities. Rather than face those fears, many individuals would rather lower their expectations, back off, and make concessions.

Con artists and manipulators love arrogant people. Because arrogant people have not confronted their fears, they can be easily manipulated. **If we do not face our fears, we will not handle our**

arrogance, and the bottom-line costs can be significant. However, if we have faced our fears, no one can use them to manipulate us.

Arrogance is often a choice of being "right" at the cost of being effective. We need to watch that we don't get caught thinking, "Well, I'm right!" We certainly may be right—but it is important to keep in mind that there are many different perspectives of what that means. We need to ask ourselves if the motive behind our "position" is one based in essence values. If it is not, we need to look again at our insistence in maintaining our position.

Old patterns, based in insecurities of the past, urge us to insist on being right. We need to ask ourselves, "How am I insisting on being right?" For example, when another person objects to our viewpoint, do we really listen to the objection, or do we react by stressing our point even harder? This reaction is frustrating to both parties—and it never works.

Instead, we need to step back and realize that we are insisting on being right. Can we stop our insistence and sincerely try to listen and look at the other person's viewpoint? We don't have to agree with it, but we do need to try to see it without immediately depreciating it. Accept a new pattern that urges really listening to others. Although it may feel awkward at first, keep at it. The awkwardness will go away.

The simplest way to avoid arrogance is to start giving more real attention to the other person. Learn to listen. As we do, we communicate greater presence, sensitivity, and professionalism. We establish greater rapport. We also gain a greater wealth of information about the other person's real needs and attitudes. This will better enable us to align the other person's needs with the benefits we can offer. We are more persuasive and have a stronger foundation to be more effective (see *In-depth Probing*, Chapter 7, page 178.)

ANGER

Anger is an authentic emotion. Its positive aspect is its message that there is some irresponsibility or injustice present that needs addressing. By responsibly acting on that message, we transform the energy behind the anger into productive action.

Anger in and of itself is not destructive, but repressed, suppressed or harbored anger is. It is the repression and suppression that is destructive.

Anger is an active emotion. When repressed, it does not lie dormant within us until we are ready to work with it. Even though we may feel we are effectively repressing it, anger actively, if silently, becomes a destructive force rather than the liberating force it could be. When integrated, anger transmutes to power.

It is important to realize that anger is always processed one way or another. It is not a choice of **whether** we process anger; we do and we will. Rather, it is a case of **how** we do so. If we choose to pretend that we are not feeling anger when it exists, it will backfire and be processed either through our body in the form of disease and discomfort or in the form of problems or failures.

Confronting Why We Repress, Suppress, or Harbor Anger

All repressed, suppressed, or harbored anger (or any emotion) is a refusal to confront and take responsibility for some aspect of our behavior. We buy into the payoffs, which are always ultimately unsatisfying and unfulfilling. If we find ourselves continually upset and angry (no matter how "justified"), we need to answer the following questions:

- Why do I want to feel righteous?
- What am I avoiding?
- Who am I punishing?
- What kinds of guarantees am I still holding out for?
- Do I enjoy self-pity enough to suffocate opportunities for more gratifying interactions?

- Does being angry contribute to my feeling of self-importance?
- What do I fear I will lose if I give up my anger?

Anger's Place in Relationships

"Clean" anger never hurt anyone. It is dishonesty that hurts. If we are afraid of losing a relationship if we honestly express our feelings, it's time to look at that relationship and assess it right now in terms of how we want it to be.

Anger is an emotion, but the constructive expression of anger is a process that draws upon self-reflection, creative thinking, and effective communication skills. We need to first self-reflect about why we are angry and where our anger is coming from. Before speaking directly with someone we associate with our anger, we need to think about what we want to say and **be specific** about what we think could be solutions to our anger. We want to voice our concerns without overwhelming or being accusative toward the other person.

We need to set up a mutually convenient time and place to speak with the other person. Immediate confrontations often preclude constructive processing. We need to take responsibility and be prepared to talk about the impact of the conversation, particularly if the other person is taken by surprise or has not thought through his or her own anger. For example, if the other person lashes back or seems unwilling to talk, we need to be responsible and indicate that we want to work things out—even at a future time. Resolution may require an ongoing dialogue.

Expressing anger honestly and thoughtfully vitalizes our growth and improves the environment around us, whether at home or in the workplace, and is a measure of our emotional maturity.

Getting in touch with one's anger means we are less hidden to ourselves, more present, more aware of information that could help us respond in ways that could end our suffering. —Dalai Lama

FEELING EMOTIONS VERSUS EMOTIONALITY

Emotionality, or being emotional, is the drama—overt or covert—used to deny, cover up, and avoid listening to, feeling, and expressing real emotions. This emotionality, or acting emotional, is not actually feeling at all but rather the dramatization of repressed feeling. It is an exaggerated reaction masking other emotions such as hurt, pain, shame, anger and fear. Emotional drama is the inevitable behavioral manifestation of repressed emotions.

When we allow emotional drama to happen, we contribute to a world of socially acceptable deceit and limited expression of authentic emotions. For example, a small boy is rejected from some activity by his peer group. He feels hurt and sad and wants to cry. But he has learned that only girls cry—boys do not, boys are tough! At home, he angrily hits his younger brother and then accuses him of being a crybaby. He numbs himself to both the hurt he felt and the hurt he has caused. Repeated enough, it becomes an automatic, chronic pattern of anger, separation, and lack of empathy and compassion.

Allowing self-centered emotionality rather than feeling our real emotions severely restricts our access to the survival information real emotions provide. Repressing feelings limits honest communication and, thus, understanding. It keeps us from being empathetic to other people and closes them off to us.

In fact, any repression of feeling depletes our energy and limits our perception of what is possible. It increases our insecurities and self-centeredness, constricts our passions and dreams, and limits our choices and actions. **By repressing emotions, we effectively cut off a significant source of our power, limiting our potential to positively act and accomplish what we want.**

Encouraging the feeling and expression of emotions does not mean encouraging the dumping of hostile feelings on others. "Dumping" behavior is simply another way of avoiding the real, underlying emotions. That is being **mis-emotional,** in other words, expressing one emotion to hide, from others and ourselves, some other emotion too painful or scary to face. It is mis-emotional to express anger and blame others to cover up our underlying sense of fear, despair, or powerlessness. That kind of expression lacks authenticity and is, at minimum, unproductive and often destructive.

Being mis-emotional does not always appear to be negative. Often, we observe mis-emotion in forms that are socially acceptable. For example, we may appear pleasant and cheerful at times to hide anger, anxiety, grief or depression. That sort of mis-emotion has contributed to the social rationalization and generalization that it is better to repress than to express our true feelings.

Nevertheless, all mis-emotion is a deception, to others and to us. It ultimately restricts our choices, actions, results, and relationships. It is actual feelings, not some surrogate dramatization that generates our sense of aliveness, passion, compassion, and depth and sense of connection.

He that would be superior to external influences must first become superior to his own passions. —Samuel Johnson

WHY LIFE SEEMS A STRUGGLE

Why is it so few people seem to relish life? Why is it that so many people act weak and disempowered? **The fact is that emotional maturity and its qualities are not the norm in contemporary society.**

Constant attention to survival considerations creates the perception of a difficult, even hostile, world, where life seems more of a struggle than a joyous event. That notion is a major part of why the paradigm of "no pain, no gain" is so embedded in the current consensus reality. However, living with such a paradigm limits our power and possibilities. It is a reason why many people feel disempowered and become chronically angry, anxious, sad, or depressed. It is a major reason why so many resort to drugs—legal or otherwise—to numb the resulting physical, mental or emotional pain.

Fear-based, self-centered survival patterns are so familiar that many people feel they are natural and normal. Observing this, psychologist Abraham Maslow defined "normal" as "the average of an abberated society." Integrity and emotional maturity are often much less familiar to us and, as a result, feel relatively unnatural or abnormal.

Is life so wretched? Isn't it rather your vision which is muddled? You are the one who must grow up. —Dag Hammarskjöld

WHAT IS RAGE?

Rage is the emotional expression of feeling powerless. Rage is not just extreme anger. That is just one possible manifestation. Both anger and rage have to do with boundary issues, where either too much or too little of something is occurring. It is where boundaries are too permeable (feeling violated) or too rigid (feeling excluded or restricted) resulting in feeling powerless to do anything about our condition. When we feel powerless we have rage.

More often than not, rage lies hidden, covered by all our self-deceiving pretenses. Any time we have repressed something or allowed ourselves to be repressed, we have accumulated rage.

Many, many groups of people have been repressed, restricted, excluded and violated for centuries (for example, women, blacks, and religious minorities). They all have repressed rage. Unless enlightened, everyone has some rage, and we continue to see its manifestations in the world, ranging from simple inconsideration, to constant blaming, to child and spouse abuse, all the way to mass murder and genocide.

Rage is associated with a sense of excessive loss of value or self-worth and an intense sorrow or abject denial of shame and pain. Shame is the feeling of being defective. Pain is a synergy of separation from and longing for something. Emotional pain is a separation from and longing for belonging. Mental pain is a separation from and longing for understanding. Physical pain is a separation from and longing for control. Rather than confront all that, we repress the shame, the pain, and the rage—and we settle.

HOW WE SETTLE

We often settle for doing the same old things, simply because those things are familiar to us and familiarity makes them easier. We settle for using a few skills rather than capitalizing on the depth of our real talents. We settle for being busy rather than truly productive and lose the excitement and joy that a full sense of real productivity brings.

We settle for mediocrity rather than excellence. We become expert at justifying or denying the resultant boredom, frustration, anxiety, and sense of powerlessness. It is easier to settle into a pattern of blame and exaggeration rather than accept responsibility for and ownership of how we contributed to the situation.

Too many of us settle for pretense, feel like phonies, and would not dare act out our claims of what we are "going to do," for fear we might expose the self-perceived inadequacies we try so hard to hide. The result is that we miss out on many of our dreams and desires, which we otherwise are fully capable of living.

If unchecked, appearance rather than substance becomes our emphasis and way of life. We become insincere actors expending energy that provides little real satisfaction, regardless of our claims to the contrary.

Concern for others becomes little more than lip service. Self-centeredness reigns and is rationalized as individual initiative. Skill at one-upmanship is admired and emulated. Character and integrity are given little real weight. Material and political "success" becomes the measure of the person. Underneath it all, the sense of powerlessness builds.

We wind up leading soap opera lives, acting out someone else's script rather than authoring and directing our own story. Sometimes our rage bursts through in overtly destructive ways.

One such way is being judgmental. Judgments, in this sense, are reactive, hostile conclusions that are asserted based on previously formed ideas devoid of present-time discernment or evaluation. These "judgments" are usually projections of aspects of ourselves we reject.

One way to "cope" with feelings of being overwhelmed is to go numb. Going numb is a way of avoiding. It is a defense mechanism to dodge facing some real or imagined pain. Addictions and addictive behaviors are compulsive ways of trying to anesthetize the pain of feeling what we are afraid to face.

The stoic, unfeeling, numbed-out individual is a person who no longer has access to the whole range of emotions and to the information those emotions provide. That individual has limited survival and success potential. Greater differentiation, increased clarity of communication, enhanced survival potential, and expanded enjoyment of life all come with the healthy use of more emotions, not fewer.

High regard and a positive public image is a natural human preference. However, we will not feel satisfied or fulfilled unless we ground that image in honesty, authenticity, and real contribution. When we are dishonest about our feelings, we lose the richness that different feelings were intended to provide. We lose integrity. Rather than being in control of our lives, the "stuff out there" controls us. We increasingly become more afraid, self-centered, and defensive. To "protect" ourselves, we increasingly react, withdraw, and build higher walls. The rage builds.

When we end our repression, we regain our ability to respond to what exists. We become more responsible. We regain the perspective, confidence, passion and compassion that results owning our power. We replace our rage with a sense of calm.

Individuals whose chronic behavior is hurtful, limiting, or unloving to themselves and others have lost touch with the core of their real power—their essence values. In reacting to the perceived loss, they substitute a whole set of compensating values, beliefs, strategies, behaviors, and rationalizations that only serve to limit them further. This perceived loss is a delusion, for we cannot lose essence qualities because they are core to our very being—but we can lose touch with them. They are there—in our shadow.

THE SHADOW

The shadow is the aspect of ourselves that is the reservoir for all those things for which we are not willing or able to take responsibility. In effect, a part of us says, "I'll store this thing that seems too much for you to deal with now until you are able to take responsibility for this aspect of yourself. In effect, it is a friend, helping to keep us from being completely overwhelmed.

The things we are afraid to take responsibility for are stored in our shadow—our shadow is the sum total of all the denied aspects, positive or negative, of which we are. It is what we are capable of but will not confront. It is all those "bad" things we "could not possibly do" and those "bad" things we did do but will not own. It is all the repressed and denied rage, anger, pain, hurt and shame.

Importantly, the shadow is also the storehouse of all our denied greatness—those strengths, gifts, and talents we have not owned. It is where our repressed desire, passion, compassion, creativity, happiness, and joy reside. It is where all our unacknowledged potential lies hidden.

Some call these negative and positive aspects the dark and light shadows. Whatever the shadow is called, or however it is arbitrarily compartmentalized, the shadow is the part of us that stores all the aspects of ourselves for which we have not previously been willing to accept responsibility.

All aspects of our shadow—the light as well as the dark—must be confronted and owned before we can fully integrate them, be empowered, and feel happiness and joy. The process of owning our shadow diminishes the negative ego and builds the healthy one.

Someone asked Mother Teresa how she was able to have such a powerful impact. Her immediate response was that she had to look at and own the potential Hitler in herself. Her willingness to face her negative potential transmuted, integrated, and used that energy positively. Added to her existing positive energy, it synergistically manifested a power and effectiveness that amazed the world.

By looking at our patterns—all of them, including our dark ones—we're able to see how we run and hide and keep ourselves busy so that we never have to let our hearts be penetrated. —Pema Chödrön

THE EGO

Although often confused with the shadow, the ego is different. The ego is a survival mechanism created by humankind to replace many of the animal instincts we lost in our evolution. Animals use instincts for survival, to respond automatically without thinking. As humans developed the capacity to think, we lost our animal instincts and needed a replacement.

Consequently, we developed the ego, whose function is to be an information gatherer of what is going on "out there." It is then our responsibility to use our ability to think, to evaluate that data and take appropriate survival action.

However, when we become overwhelmed, due to trauma or other events, we increasingly avoid doing what we need to do, including evaluating data input. So, in our overwhelmed state and corresponding irresponsibility, we dump the job of evaluating on our ego.

But our ego is not equipped to evaluate and make decisions. It is only able to gather data. When we demand it do something of which it is incapable, it becomes overwhelmed, and, just as we do when we feel overwhelmed, it fights the perceived oppressor—in this case, ourselves. It attacks, in one form or another, in the interest of survival.

Thus, by being irresponsible, we create a negative ego. Our ego, instead of being a helpful servant, is now out to get us. We have given away our power of choice to our ego and wind up falsely believing that we really have no choice about many things.

Although we do not want a negative ego, we need a healthy ego. In fact, a well-functioning ego is necessary for emotional maturity to develop.

A CRY FOR LOVE

All dysfunctional behavior—no matter how despicable, hurtful or destructive—is, at its very foundation, a cry for love. The key to being responsible in the face of dysfunctional behavior is to realize that although someone else's actions may be unacceptable, that person is in pain. The more hurtful the behavior someone exhibits, the more that person is hurting. He is projecting that hurt as a defense. In that reactive and, thus, irrational state, the person is behaving in ways that produce the opposite of what he or she both needs and truly wants. The more hurtful the behavior, the more the person needs and is craving love.

Creating and maintaining appropriate boundaries around dysfunctional behavior is integral to mature, healthy behavior. Boundaries can be too open or too closed. An example of a too open boundary is an individual having difficulty saying no to additional assignments when already overloaded. Another example is an unwillingness to exclude negative people from one's environment. Boundaries that are too closed are just as dysfunctional. In this scenario, those individuals say no too often and do not say yes enough. They exclude things and people that could contribute to their well-being. We all need boundaries. Otherwise, we would be overwhelmed. However, we need to keep them in perspective and balance.

When dealing with dysfunctional behavior, it is important to remain empathetic and compassionate to the underlying cry for love while also maintaining appropriate boundaries. Integrating both is a measure of our ability to be truly responsive versus reactive. That facility is an indication of our emotional maturity and is a critical component of effective, powerful leadership.

SO YOU WANT TO BE HAPPY

"Happiness" can be defined as getting our needs met and "joy" as getting our preferences met. What do we really want in our lives? What are our needs? What are our preferences? What are the qualities and characteristics of those needs and preferences? Do we know the difference? How do we get there?

The steps to getting there are the same as the qualities of being there. Correspondingly, the qualities of being there are the same as the steps to getting there. If we want more honesty and love in our life, we need to be more honest and loving. It can be that simple. If we are not experiencing the qualities we say we want, it behooves us to look honestly at our willingness to truly be and have those qualities in our life.

Unhappiness or discontent has at its core an unwillingness to be present with something. We can't be happy when we're not present. Being discontent or unhappy with anything simply means there is something we do not want to deal with, something we do not want to face.

Why? Because there is something present that re-stimulates some false sense of deficiency—some sense of not being up to the task of dealing with it. However, by not confronting that lie, it sticks, and we wind up believing it and spend our lives trying to compensate for it.

We believe that "something better," that is, happiness, connection, and fulfillment, is "out there"—separate from ourselves. That basic lie—that "better" is separate—is what traps us in a chronic sense of "not being good enough." It is what sticks us in our compulsive compensations.

As long as we believe better is "out there," not "in here," it will remain so, and we will never have a sense of attaining it—no matter how hard we try. As long as we spend our efforts trying to perfect our compensations, we will always feel inadequate.

No matter how skillful our compensations, how much we gain through them, or how much they are acknowledged and admired by the outside world, they never will be enough. We will experience pain and suffering, in the form of disconnection and separation, and we will perpetuate a limiting, impoverished perspective.

When we recognize that what we want and must deal with is all "in here"—not "out there," and when we accept that we are responsible for our own condition, then we can let go of the limiting and misdirected compensations. Only then, are we fully capable of owning our power, being empowered, and being happy more of the time.

To the degree that we are willing to feel our feelings and appropriately express them, we open the door to increasing responsibility for what transpires in our lives. Doing so is a choice away.

Winning and losing are about attitudes and perceptions. We choose them. We are either the cause or the effect. Pick one. Being happy or unhappy is a choice, our choice. When we own that it is our choice and only our choice, we no longer feel controlled and victimized by the "stuff out there." We increasingly expand our ability to responsibly make needed changes, do what needs being done and manifest what we truly need and want. Doing this is being emotionally mature. Only then can true happiness and joy be a continuing part of our lives.

In the following chapter, we take a deeper look at emotional maturity as a foundation to happiness and effective leadership.

5
Emotional Maturity

For all of man's evolution and considerable technological accomplishments, psychologically he is still very immature.
— Krishnamurti

DEFINING EMOTIONAL MATURITY

Emotional maturity is a balance between a healthy ego identity, that is, a sense of being an autonomous individual, and an ability and willingness to relate to others in an authentic and meaningful way. It means being willing and able to integrate independence with interdependence and to responsibly confront and deal with all the issues of life—the "bad" as well as the "good." It is about ending the blame and owning the "stuff" for which we avoid responsibility. It is living essence values and doing so spontaneously. In other words, emotional maturity is acting with integrity. **Emotionally mature people see their lives as a sequence of personal choices for which they are singularly responsible.**

The development of emotional maturity relates directly to the stages of ego development. Each stage's respective focus of attention are as follows:

Stage 1: Infant/Young Child—"Am I getting enough?"

Stage 2: Child/Young Adolescent—"Am I good enough?"

Stage 3: Adolescent/Young Adult—"Am I being, doing, having, learning, growing enough?"

Stage 4: Mature Adult—"I am enough."

We all need to experience these stages. Each stage provides a necessary learning experience that needs integration as part of the growing up/maturing process. It is the process of going from being totally dependent (Stage 1), to the gradual breaking of that dependency (Stage 2), to a sense of autonomous independence (Stage 3), to inclusive interdependence (Stage 4).

The self is not something ready-made, but something in continuous formation through choice of action. —John Dewey

If any stage is not allowed to develop fully, the needed learning is not integrated, and an individual tends to become emotionally stuck in that stage. For example, sometimes parents expect or demand (for their own immature ego needs) that their child act like an adult before the child is ready. One common resulting manifestation is that later in life the child, who is now an adult, has little sense of play and often feels that she has not yet grown up but needs to pretend she is, making her feel like a phony in the process. Another common reaction to a child having missed their play years is as an adult compensating for that loss by inappropriately acting childish in present time. In fact, many older people are stuck in one of the earlier stages of ego development. These people can spend a great deal of energy concerned about fixing something they sense is not as it should be, yet unclear exactly what that is. This too adds to an uncomfortable sense of a lack of authenticity.

Stifled ego development offers a partial explanation for why we observe so much dysfunctional, self-serving behavior. The behaviors we generally see, and those that are so often rewarded, are not those of honesty, authenticity and collaboration but their opposites. Collaborative behavior, a characteristic of a mature ego, seems to be a rarity too often given little more than lip service. Instead, we place an overly heavy emphasis on competition and the accumulation of material possessions, typical of an adolescent perception of needs and priorities. Achievement in competition and material accumulation appears to be the primary measure of success in much of society.

There is nothing inherently wrong with competition or accumulation of material possessions. Their impact, "good" or "bad," depends on whether it is interpreted from a mature perspective. Competition among individuals functioning from a mature adult ego brings out creative juices and produces a challenging learning environment that tends to manifest as an innovative, dynamic expansion of possibilities. Competition among people in any other stage is predictably self-serving and problematic. It is often destructive and always rationalized. This is simply another reason why it imperative that raising the emotional maturity of the organization be a senior management priority.

Maslow's *Hierarchy of Needs* describes the needs of human beings in dealing with the issues they must confront in both growing up and life in general. It corresponds to the stages of ego development (see Table 5.1, page 116). All those needs are continually present; only their emphasis changes. As physical beings, we have survival and security needs. As relational beings, we have belonging needs. As contributing beings, we have esteem needs. As evolving, growing beings, we have actualizing needs. They are all human needs, but keeping them in balance and perspective is a must.

Our needs change with time and context. What those needs are depends largely on our perceptions, which are based primarily on our emotional state. Those needs continue to recycle throughout life. Each time they offer an opportunity to expand our awareness and ability. We will not progress to the next stage of ego development until we have fully confronted the needs of the current stage. Part of the learning, developing, maturing process is to gain experience in what works and what does not work in getting those needs met. Each stage has lessons that must be learned and integrated before moving on. Those "grown-ups" we observe acting like children or adolescents much of the time have not confronted some needed lesson of one of the earlier stages. When those fears are confronted we are then able to move on to the next stage. By so doing, we begin meeting ours needs in an increasingly elegant (maximum effect for the least amount of effort) manner.

TABLE 5.1

Correlation of the Stages of Ego Development and Maslow's Hierarchy of Needs

Stages of Ego Development	Maslow's Hierarachy of Needs
Mature Adult *"I am enough."*	Self-Actualization
Adolescent/Young Adult *"Am I learning, doing, growing, being enough?"*	Esteem
	Belonging
Child/Young Adolescent *"Am I good enough?"*	Security
Infant/Young Child *"Am I getting enough?*	Survival

The further along people are in the stages of ego development, the more easily and elegantly they can handle the needs of the lower stages (survival, security, belonging), as those needs arise in the give-and-take of life. The mature adult deals with those needs as a part of life but doesn't become stuck in them. An overemphasis on any one of those needs, to the exclusion or minimization of the others, creates an imbalance in dealing with the wholeness of life. Being chronically out of balance, for example a workaholic, is an indication of something avoided, denied, or repressed. The resulting workaholic behavior is little more than a compulsive compensation. Until that denial or repression is confronted, that individual will not advance to the next ego stage, regardless of financial, social or political "success." Observe how many people are chronically irritable or depressed, and how many focus much of their attention on losses or regrets of the past or fears about the future. Notice how few have the courage to live their dreams in the present. These people have not attained adult ego maturity. This not about judgments of good or bad, right or wrong. Rather it is an observation of who are less happy, less passionate, feeling less fulfilled about the life they are living than they could be.

A primary characteristic of mature people is that when survival, security, belonging or esteem issues manifest, they deal with them in a responsive manner versus the defensive, reactionary manner that results from an insecure, immature ego state. Mature people consistently demonstrate a resiliency to restoring a positive balance to their environment. They are continually learning from each experience, regardless of the label of "good" or "bad" placed on it. Immature people are reactive, less resilient, have difficultly learning from their experiences, and are more resistant to change. Mature people create positive change of substance.

Society's emphasis on appearance, at the expense of substance, and the pretenses and façades that such emphasis encourages, often makes it difficult to grasp an individual's actual level of emotional maturity and stage of ego development. One of the best ways to make an assessment is simply to observe what ego behavior the person reverts to when **under stress.** They will manifest the behaviors and attitudes of one of the four stages described above. In current society, the Mature Adult Stage is the least likely to be present. Most often we observe that the type of need an individual reveals (such as security or belonging) will correspond to its parallel ego stage as indicated in Table 5.1.

Dr. Frederick Herzberg studied the factors involved in getting people to accomplish tasks. He found two main categories, one of which he called **motivational factors**—factors that propelled people toward accomplishment. The second he called hygiene or **maintenance factors**—factors needed to keep people on the job.

For example, a person's salary must be sufficient to meet her survival needs. Once those needs are met, other things become more important. Although we may all like a bigger salary, for most of us salary is primarily a maintenance factor not a motivational factor.

According to Herzberg, personal growth is a much higher motivational factor than salary or working conditions. However, just as with the stages of ego development and Maslow's Hierarchy of Needs, lower order needs must be met sufficiently before higher-order considerations can even come into play. Herzberg's factors appear to correspond closely with both the stages of ego development and Maslow's Hierarchy of Needs (see Table 5.2).

TABLE 5.2

Correlation of the Stages of Ego Development, Maslow's Hierarchy of Needs and Herzberg's Two-Factor Job Model

Stages of Ego Development	Maslow's Hierarachy of Needs	Herzberg's Two-Factor Job Model
Mature Adult "*I am enough.*"	Self-Actualization	<u>Motivational Factors</u> Growth Potential Responsibility Achievement Recognition Advancement
Adolescent/Young Adult "*Am I learning, doing, growing, being enough?*"	Esteem	
		<u>Maintenance Factors</u> Interpersonal Relations—Peers, Supervisors, Subordinates
Child/Young Adolescent "*Am I good enough?*"	Belonging	
		Company Policy
	Security	Job Security
Infant/Young Child "*Am I getting enough?*"		Work Conditions
	Survival	Salary

Developing greater emotional maturity is a process of expanding our willingness and ability to be responsible and accountable for our choices and behaviors. Illuminating the elements and dynamics of that process is a primary purpose of this book.

For many people, the process of ego development is retarded. Despite outward social measures of success, many people have not grown

up emotionally. Emotionally, many are still children or adolescents occupying older bodies. Behind their social façades, they demonstrate the same insecurities, concerns, and considerations of limitations as do children or adolescents. Think about how many adults you know who, when under a little stress, automatically revert to behavior similar to that of a spoiled child or teenager. When that occurs, which may be often, decisions, choices made, and actions taken are on a correspondingly immature level.

As we move from emotional naiveté and immaturity toward being more emotionally intelligent and mature, correspondingly we develop a greater sense of security. This manifests in behaviors that are less self-centered, more honest, authentic, and responsible more of the time. Communication and interpersonal effectiveness dramatically expand. This obviously can have a dramatic effect on organizational effectiveness as well as personal happiness. This maturation process is a learning, growing, sometimes exciting, sometimes frustrating experience, always a little scary and confusing, but, if not repressed, enormously fulfilling.

THE GENESIS OF LIMITATION

Limiting behaviors originate from limiting beliefs. Our beliefs form the basis of our experiences and how we perceive ourselves and the world around us. When those beliefs are limited, we limit our perception and experience of what is possible. It doesn't matter if those beliefs are false. As long as we believe them, they will accordingly impact and mold our perception of experience. The more limiting our beliefs, the less powerful we falsely sense ourselves to be. Actually, any beliefs, even the "noble" ones, narrow our focus and are limiting and restrictive.

The **universal core delusion** that initiates our limiting behaviors is a **delusion of insignificance;** that is, not feeling good enough. Some form of trauma— physical, mental, emotional, or spiritual— during which we felt overwhelmed and helpless often triggers this delusion. Trauma is anything that keeps a person from fully experiencing, integrating, and responding to what is occurring in the moment. The result of trauma is that we severely narrow and limit our focus to defensive survival behaviors. We react rather than respond.

With each trauma, we feel more helpless. We further narrow our focus, and may do so to such an extent that we believe ourselves to be insignificant. Each of us tries in our own unique way to compensate for that feeling of insignificance. We develop sophisticated strategies to deal with our sense of not being good enough. We create masks (personality traits) to hide a stressful feeling of inadequacy from ourselves as well as others.

Initially, those strategies were survival mechanisms that appeared to deal with the situation or provide some stress relief. When that stress reappeared, we again used what seemed to work in the past. Eventually, those strategies became unconscious, automatic defense patterns we use reactively when anything even resembling the original trauma or stress reappears. We start to identify with the pattern: "That's who I am. Doing anything different just wouldn't be me." Letting go of that pattern, of that identification, feels like losing or abandoning a part of ourselves; hence, the understandable reluctance to give it up. **All limiting beliefs are self-sustained.**

The major problem is that this unconscious, reactive behavior shuts out discernment of the actual present-time situation, limiting, if not eliminating, an appropriate response. However, because our considerations are a delusion, in trying to compensate for that delusion, we are trying to solve a problem that fundamentally does not exist. Therefore, any compensating behavior(s), no matter how brilliantly achieved and acknowledged, will never be sufficient. By remaining fixated on the delusion, the need becomes insatiable, demanding increasingly more energy and attention. We gradually become depleted—physically, mentally, and emotionally. This process of deterioration impairs our ability to communicate authentically and be happy.

Remember, no one can make you feel inferior, or anything else, without your consent. —Eleanor Roosevelt

THE SPIRAL OF DETERIORATION

As stress increases, our compensations become more intense and irrational. Being able to see the big picture and manifest abundance, ease, elegance, happiness and joy progressively deteriorates, first into a somewhat more conservative and narrower outlook. If the stress continues, so does the deterioration. We begin to manifest overt forms of opposition, in the form of antagonism, anger, and blame. As our fear increases, we regress to passive–aggressive behavior and covert hostility. The bottom of the spiral of deterioration goes from fear to a sense of loss and, finally, to despair and apathy.

As we deteriorate, our perspectives become narrower and more fixated. Our sense of being able to cope with life diminishes. More and more, we perceive the world as hostile, to be defended against or avoided. Our desperation intensifies. We increasingly replace responsibility, honesty, trustworthiness, and happiness with their opposites. We wind up feeling out of control and powerless and attempt to compensate by assuming control and power over others. Our behaviors become more irrational, dysfunctional, unworkable and destructive. The results of these behaviors are the opposite of what we actually need.

As we honestly recognize where we are in our deterioration and face our immature behaviors, we are then—and only then—in a position to reverse the process.

THE MATURATION PROCESS

The maturation process is the reverse of the deterioration process described above. It includes an increasing willingness to face our fears and take responsibility for our current and previously disowned behaviors. It also includes an increasing willingness to own more of our inherent strengths, gifts, and talents—and to act on them. Ultimately, it is the individual's choice to grow up.

Paradoxically, it is when we reject something that our attention becomes fixated on it. When we are willing to view and own what we have been denying, we release the fixated attention. We feel lighter and more open. We can then see and own our full range of capabilities, from our dark shadow to our bright potential. Then we are willing to take on those qualities and behaviors most helpful in balancing our previously blind area.

Emotional intelligence requires more than intellectual knowledge of emotional dynamics. To respond effectively to life situations, we must integrate both cognitive and emotional awareness. Thinking and feeling are meant to work together, to support and add clarity to each other. Emotional intelligence and cognitive intelligence go hand in hand. We cannot think without feeling, and we cannot feel without thinking. One without the other is insufficient. It lacks wholeness. It lacks integrity. Together, they create a synergy of greater awareness, producing more responsible, fulfilling choices and actions. When either thinking or feeling is repressed, this synergy of expanded awareness evaporates. The more we responsibly integrate and use our thoughts and feelings in dealing with life situations, the more we move toward emotional maturity.

Human beings, by changing the inner attitudes of their minds, can change the outer aspects of their lives. —William James

EMOTIONAL MATURITY IS A CONSCIOUS CHOICE

As helpful as understanding emotional dynamics can be, that knowledge does not automatically make a person emotionally mature. Nor does emotional maturity happen because we reach a certain age, have a job, get married, have children, make lots of money, or attain a high social or political position. Genes and hormones drive children and adolescents. However, **beyond adolescence we have to consciously choose maturity. Emotional maturity is a result of conscious choice—our conscious choice to be responsible for our impact.** If we do not make this choice, we will not move beyond the emotional immaturity of an adolescent, despite any trappings of material success. Once past adolescence, we can choose to be emotionally mature, with all the power and freedom that maturity provides.

Self-centeredness and self-importance are characteristics of children and adolescents, who expect to be taken care of without exchange, demand special treatment, and complain that life is not meeting their demands. This does not make them bad. It is simply part of the maturation process. However, these behaviors are not characteristics of emotionally mature individuals. When they manifest chronically in a grown-up, they are indications that that person is not a mature, responsive adult. Rather, he is still reacting out of the behavioral patterns of the self-centered child or self-important adolescent.

There are a great many people who look grown up and appear to be successful by contemporary standards, who are emotionally still children or adolescents. Perhaps they were overly influenced by dysfunctional parents who had no idea how to model responsible mature behavior. If the only adult models they experienced were reactive ones, it is likely that they will model similar behavior or its reactive counterpart. Regardless of the reason, they are people caught in reactive behavior who erroneously view maturity and responsibility as burdens to be avoided.

Reactive behavior is always inappropriate in dealing with present circumstances. When an adult acts reactively, the reactive pattern often originated early in childhood, when the individual had little experience or guidance in developing adequate defense mechanisms. Unless a person's childhood environment was unusually mature and appropriately supportive and nurturing, the person usually lacks a fundamental sense of security. The common result is that the individual "grows up" with a compensatory need for what often becomes an insatiable fixation on substitute symbols for security, such as money, status, power, prestige, approval, or acceptance.

Grounded in a fundamental sense of security, personal empowerment and self-esteem, the emotionally mature adult does not need compensatory symbols of success. He or she may prefer them and have them but does not need them. He or she may prefer to be accepted but does not need to be accepted.

Therapists speak of the need for letting go of the past and interrupting habituated, dysfunctional patterns. By interrupting dysfunctional patterns of the past and breaking their grip on us, we are more available to be present, to discern, evaluate, and choose actions that optimize and empower us. In order to let go of our dysfunctional patterns, we first need to recognize them. However, because all change generates confusion, doubt, and fear, we often resist even seeing anything that would cause us to give up our familiar patterns—even when they are blatantly ruining our lives. So we keep doing what is familiar—choosing "the devil we know over the devil we don't"—hoping that it will somehow create a different result. This is why change, individually or organizationally, is usually so difficult and resisted even when obviously needed.

Truly growing up, becoming emotionally mature, is about letting go of the past, being in the now, and responding, not reacting, to what is. Hanging onto the past becomes a convenient way to scapegoat and blame parents, others, and life situations for our problems and relationship issues. We use scapegoats to avoid facing our own irresponsible, immature behaviors. Instead of being responsive to what is, we are reactive to what was and are thus less able to appropriately deal with what is.

A fundamental part of the route from adolescence to adult maturity is letting go of blaming others for our pain. Blame is about hanging onto unresolved grievances and irresponsibilities of the past. We need to learn to forgive ourselves as well as others before we can take charge of our life in the present.

Our parents may not have been exemplary, and they did have a significant impact on us. Some of that impact was less than ideal. Some may have been very hurtful and destructive. However, that was then and this is **now!** We have to ask honestly, who is re-creating the issue now? Is hanging on to upsets and resentments of the past worth the cost we are paying physically, mentally and emotionally?

Alas, after a certain age, every man is responsible for his own face.
—Albert Camus

We ought not to look back unless it is to derive useful lessons from past errors, and for the purpose of profiting by dear bought experience.
—George Washington

WILLINGNESS—THE DETERMINING FACTOR

Power is the ability and willingness to act. Both must be present. When you have no power to get something accomplished, sometimes it is simply a lack of ability, but more often than not, it's a lack of willingness. In most cases, if we're truly willing, we can develop the necessary abilities or resources.

Willingness is the determining factor of our power, empowerment, success, abundance, wealth, prosperity, health, and happiness. Our willingness or lack thereof sets the boundaries of our reality. To expand those boundaries, we need to review our willingness.

Often we base our sense of "deservability" or "worthiness" on what we do or have. We make judgments about who is deserving enough or worthy enough, including ourselves. Such judgments not only indicate our biases but also are simply not valid. On a fundamental level, we all deserve and we all are worthy. No matter how hard we try or how much we achieve, nothing we accomplish will ever make us any more worthy or deserving that we already are.

Our sense of personal empowerment and happiness is based on our willingness to recognize and acknowledge our **inherent** deservability and worth. It is from our willingness that we create or allow any and all manifestations.

What Are We Willing to Be, Do, and Have?

What are we willing to be? What are we willing to do? What are we willing to have? What are we not willing to be, do, and have? Are we willing to do what is necessary to develop the skills and resources to be, do, and have what we say we want? Part of emotional maturity is honestly looking at what we are and are not willing to be, do, and have. Are we willing to:

- Be present with whatever is present, including our fears?
- Be authentic and honest (with ourselves and others)? Own our personal shadow?
- Allow others their viewpoint, attitude, and position (even if we do not agree with them)?
- Own our power?
- Give ourselves permission to act?
- Assume our authority to act?
- Do the right thing just because it's the right thing?
- Persist through the inevitable resistances to change (act with commitment, determination and resolve)?
- Recognize and be responsible for our impact?

It takes willingness to:

- Face the confusion, doubt, and fear inherent in any real change;

- Reconsider our cultural bias, which emphasizes appearance over substance;
- Own how we're contributing to that bias;
- Face and persist through the awkward phase of learning how to do something different;
- Recognize and act on more of our inherent strengths and talents;
- Put concepts and ideas into action; and,
- Allow ourselves to manifest and have what we truly want.

Since patterns of behavior are largely unconscious and automatic, we tend to see and hear primarily within that automatic framework. Thus, we fail to hear when other people try to tell us, nicely or otherwise, that perhaps we are causing some harm by our actions or ways of relating. As we become more willing to hear, face, and go through our fears, we are often surprised, even astounded, to realize how blind we have been to the harm we have caused, allowed, or contributed to. This is the "gulp phase." This is what we would rather not face, but it is exactly what we must see and accept if we are to change and grow.

The worst thing we can do to ourselves is let our fears control our willingness to look at ourselves honestly. The more we disown, the more we give away our power. The more we become victims, the more we need to create justifications and rationalizations, such as "There's nothing I can do about it—that's the way it is. That's reality."

We cannot get where we really want to go without being aware of our own habits and patterns. Thus, growth is a process of being increasingly willing to peel back, expose, and take responsibility for the layers of our own self-deception. If we are not willing to face our fears and persist through the inevitable resistance, fear and resistance will control our lives. To the degree we are willing and have courage and commitment, we can put ourselves back in control of our lives.

If we are willing to face all of our patterns, including the less-than-desirable ones, we can then see how we deceive others and ourselves and limit our happiness and ourselves. Recognizing other people's patterns is helpful. Recognizing our own is vital. The willingness to be present with whatever is present—the "good" and the "bad"—is the crucial starting point. It enables us to be more consciously aware of what we are actually creating in the midst of everyday situations and challenges.

The bottom-line question is how willing are we to be honest with ourselves? When we are willing to face and own our patterns, they can no longer run our lives, and our universe of freedom and choice expands.

Every individual has a place to fill in the world, and it is important whether he chooses to do so or not. —Nathaniel Hawthorne

BLAME

Blame has nothing to do with honest assessment of cause. It is a reactive denial and an exaggerated projection of cause. When people blame others, they are, in effect, saying, "I'm not responsible—someone else is." Blame implies a victim, that is, "I'm innocent and have been abused." The behavior, being reactive versus responsive, is disproportionate to the problem and accusatory in tone. With blame, there is no constructive action, only complaining, whining, or aggressive behavior.

It may be true that we have been unjustly treated in a situation. However, far too often we use the fact of another person's irresponsible behavior as a distraction from looking at our part in allowing or creating the situation. A blaming reaction to someone else's behavior is often an attempt to deny—to ourselves as well as others—how we have contributed to or allowed some unacceptable behavior. Blaming is using other people's irresponsibility to deny and distract us from aspects of ourselves for which we have not yet owned responsibility.

Whenever we blame, we disown something, lose our integrity and give away our power. It is the intensity of the blaming reaction, versus constructive responding, that hints at the degree of denial present. This reactive behavior, denying any ownership of responsibility, severely limits the blamer's potential for making any real change: "You can't sell it if you don't own it." That is why people who blame others will often stay upset and angry, sometimes for years. Their denial of any ownership of responsibility precludes constructive change and keeps their anger intact.

One ought to examine himself for a very long time before thinking of condemning others. —Molière

FROM BLAME TO RESPONSIBILITY—THE KEY TO POWER AND EMPOWERMENT

A powerful exercise is to look at what and how we blame. The faults we find in others are often indicators of what we need to look at in ourselves. If we are willing, we can use what we are upset about as a reflection to help us identify and own some aspect of ourselves that we are denying or have not recognized before.

We are responsible for our impact. Others are responsible for their impact. The more of our impact we recognize and take responsibility for, the more empowered we become. If we are willing to use what upsets us as a mirror to look deeper and to take more responsibility for our impact, we open the door to expanded awareness, growth, and empowerment.

We need to recognize and own our piece of a situation—no more, no less. Denying any of our impact, no matter how large or small, positive or negative, is disempowering to ourselves. Our willingness to observe, confront, and own our part is where the opportunities for growth, maturity and personal empowerment lie.

We should every night call ourselves to an account. Our vices will abate of themselves if they are brought every day to the shaft. —Seneca

The Gulp Stage

If we are upset and are, in effect, judging negatively what that person did or did not do, we need to ask how have we done some form of "that" ourselves. There is something of a similar nature, or mirror image, that we have not recognized or owned before. When we are mis-emotional about someone else's behavior, inevitably we are hiding something from ourselves. For example, if we find ourselves feeling upset with and blaming someone because he or she did not follow through as promised, it is an opportunity to look closer at how we have not been fully responsible for our own promised or implied follow-through. This is often the "gulp stage," for it is here that we finally recognize how irresponsible we have been.

It may very well be true that another person was irresponsible and didn't deliver as promised—and that may need to be dealt with—but **the opportunity and the empowering aspect is our increased willingness to recognize and take more ownership of the impact of our own behavior.**

When we shift our attention from how the other person is upsetting us (placing responsibility "out there") to how we are doing something similar and have been denying it (placing responsibility "in here"), three things immediately occur:

- We are less upset (our attention has shifted from blame to being more responsible);
- We have more positive control—we shifted our focus and intention from where we had little control (the other person) to where we have greater control (ourselves);
- We feel lighter and more empowered (the inevitable result of taking increased responsibility for our own behavior).

Going deeper is an opportunity not only to observe an aspect of our impact for which we have not been taking responsibility, but also to recognize the pattern of how we have been avoiding responsibility. Only when we are able to recognize and own our pattern are we able to drop the victim attitude. Only then are we able to be more personally responsible, expand our options and choices and empower ourselves to manifest constructive change.

The elegance of this process is that it is not dependent on the "rightness" or "wrongness" of either party. It is dependent solely on our willingness to observe and take responsibility for our own part in creating or allowing the upsetting situation to occur.

When you see a man of the highest caliber, give thought to obtaining his stature. When you see one who is not, go home and conduct a self-examination. —Confucius

THE DIFFERENCE BETWEEN EMOTIONALLY HEALTHY AND EMOTIONALLY UNHEALTHY PEOPLE

A measure of an individual's emotional health and maturity is not that the person always feels good, but rather that he or she has the ability and willingness to recognize, confront, and own the emotion he or she is experiencing, including the "not so nice" emotions.

Becoming more emotionally mature is about becoming more consciously aware of and taking greater personal responsibility for the choices we make and the impact those choices have. Emotions are the communication that provides the basis for differentiation and discernment of what that impact is. Our emotional health reflects our ability to be authentically responsive to the entire hierarchy of emotions. Real feelings, when not repressed, expedite greater clarity, certainty, and focus. They help us take greater responsibility for ourselves and our environment.

Healthy, emotionally mature people are more able to face and deal with whatever is present in the moment. The healthier a person, the greater his or her ability and flexibility in feeling and appropriately expressing the entire span of emotions, from apathy and despair to enthusiasm and bliss. The healthy person feels joy at a friend's success, fear when a bull charges, anger at injustice, and grief over the loss of a loved one. Healthy people feel the feeling, "get the message," and convert the emotional energy into positive action. They are able and willing to respond to the situation at hand. They are aware of and accountable for the impact they create. They are correspondingly more resilient, reliable and trustworthy in dealing with all situations, including negative ones. Communication between emotionally mature people is much more honest and effective. Therefore, contribution and real productivity expand. Increased morale follows when people feel they are contributing and productive.

Do emotionally mature people get angry? Of course. They get angry at incompetence, irresponsibility, injustice, and destructive, manipulative behavior. However, they are not reactive in their anger. They do not identify with the emotion. Rather, they acknowledge it and are responsive to it (that is, they realize the anger is a message that something is wrong in the environment, and they responsibly act on it). The energy of their anger is quickly transformed into constructive, appropriately forceful corrective action.

Do emotionally mature individuals feel grief? Again, of course. But they don't try to repress it. They allow themselves to experience the sadness and the emptiness it represents. They are honest with themselves about their feelings. This honesty is what allows them to move beyond their grief. They may always miss the object of their loss, but they are not consumed by it. They can move on and see life as full of opportunities for learning and growth.

Similarly, emotionally mature people face their fears. In fact, they have a willingness and ability to confront and learn from their experience of the entire range of emotions and their messages. This is where real courage resides.

Immature people do not "listen to the messages." They are less willing to experience the entire span of emotions. They repress the "uncomfortable" emotions, often projecting those very feelings onto others, or they arrogantly rationalize ignoring them as "inappropriate." Since they are relatively unwilling to deal with what is, their lack of responsiveness translates into a correspondingly reduced ability and resiliency to recover from any stressful situation. They remain in an overwhelmed and dysfunctional state much longer. To compensate, they further project responsibility onto and blame others.

As this dwindling spiral of irresponsibility continues, they limit their ability to learn, change, and grow. Their chronic emotional state stays negative and limiting. They tend to perceive life as a series of frustrations and limitations. Authentic communication is replaced with glibness and lies. Real productivity is replaced with busywork and pretense.

We all have our ups and downs in dealing with life. We acutely experience (unless we repress) the entire range of emotions and their associated behaviors. However, the emotionally mature person is responsive rather than reactive. Thus, the mature person deals with occasional dysfunctional attitudes and behaviors expeditiously.

The degree to which an individual is chronically reactive rather than responsive is the degree, regardless of social appearances, of that person's emotional immaturity. To most of life's pressures, the average person tends to be more reactive than responsive. In this reactivity, insecurity rules. This creates jealousy, envy, and rage. The accompanying manifestations are self-centeredness, defensiveness, lack of authenticity, social pretense, sabotaging behavior, greed, restricted choice, and unhappiness. A sign of immaturity is the degree to which those factors chronically dominate a person's attitudes and behaviors. To the degree they do, that person treats others as either threats or needed sources of approval or gratification. An emotionally mature adult is not controlled by such factors.

The mature person is one who recognizes that challenges encountered in life are part of the continuing learning and growing process. He or she is both willing and able to deal with those challenges responsibly. Emotionally healthy people do not always feel good, but their overall outlook on life is positive. They enjoy themselves and others while recognizing their own and other's foibles. They deal with problem situations directly, take responsibility for their mistakes, learn from them, and move on to a higher, more productive manner of living.

Part of being mature is recognizing what needs to be done and doing it. It is being able to appreciate and enjoy the nuances of the process even when the process is not ideal. Mature people do not demand instant gratification, as would a child, or only see things as adolescents tend to, as black or white, good or bad, pleasure or pain. Mature people face and deal with all of life, including the problems, responsibly. They do learn from experience and consciously eliminate old patterns that no longer work.

When we confront and own what makes us tick—including our darker side—the things we were afraid to face usually turn out to be less threatening than we believed them to be. However, if we do not confront them, they become a liability and be quite dangerous.

The more we confront, the more we recognize our inherent power. We see more of our potential. As we do so, we see that we have greater choice in everything we do and in everything we have. We also become more aware of the real power that greater choice allows. We begin to honor ourselves more. Our sense of self-respect and self-esteem soars. Our self-image expands. We no longer need to create problems just to avoid looking at what is really there. We can stop our unique form of compulsiveness, whether it is overeating, overworking, or "over-" or "under-" anything. In other words, we stop harming and sabotaging ourselves and others. We start appreciating ourselves and others more, and we start using more of our inherent strengths and talents. We honor our values, principles and commitments. Things are no longer as upsetting as they used to be. When issues do arise, we deal with them much more directly and expeditiously. We see much more humor in the circumstances of life. A sense of balanced perspective is more easily a larger part of our lives. We begin living life with more passion and compassion. We have more vitality. We become emotionally mature beings of character and integrity.

Happiness does not depend on outward things but on the way we see them. —Leo Tolstoy

STARTING THE FLOW

Anyone who wants or needs to get things done that requires the assistance of others knows that one of our most valuable assets is the willingness of other people to help. It is important to be able to distinguish the willing person from the unwilling person. Temporary upset can be confused with unwillingness. Willingness is measured by observable contributions. No contribution equals little or no willingness, regardless of a person's excuses, justifications, or rationalizations.

Beyond being able to differentiate the willing from the unwilling, the ability to create, develop, and preserve willingness in others is foundational to generating an attitude and culture of service to others. In order to develop willingness in others, we must first be willing to help them with their needs. (See *In-Depth Probing*, Chapter 7, page 178 and *The Value of Competent Coaching*, Chapter 8, page 205.) Far too often we don't think about the needs of others and only communicate when we want something from them. We expect, and sometimes demand, a flow of willingness when we have done little or nothing to earn it. How willing have we been, and how willing are we to be helpful? Without some ulterior motive, how often do we ask and mean, "How can I help you?" How often do we observe someone needing something and just provide it? How often have we been thanked for our helpfulness?

Willingness creates willingness. If we are willing to help others, they tend to be willing to help us. Therefore, we need to take the initiative. We need to start the flow. Being interested in and listening to the viewpoints, feelings, needs, and aspirations of others is key. By doing so, we help create and preserve people's sense of importance and value. This in turn creates the foundation of willingness.

We establish the communication. **We** find out what others need and provide it to the best of our ability and resources. Our emphasis should be on others' needs, not our own. It should be on outflow rather than inflow, on giving, not receiving.

Occasionally, we will experience people who just take and never give, but for the most part, our willingness to help will generate a reciprocal behavior in others. If we are honestly willing to be present and interested, to listen, to evaluate, and to responsibly help satisfy other people's needs, we will start the process of developing a willingness in others to do the same. Are you willing to start the flow? Suggested reading: *Robert K. Greenleaf: A Life of Servant Leadership* by Don M. Frick.

Maturity begins to grow when you can sense your concern for others outweighing your concern for yourself. —John McNaughton

Only a life lived in the service to others is worth living. —Albert Einstein

REVIEW

We live in a dynamic, continually evolving universe where change is the sole constant. How effective we are in dealing with change directly impacts our sense of well-being and happiness.

Change creates challenges. Depending on our perspective, those challenges will be regarded as either opportunities or problems. Which perspective we assume is largely determined by our level of emotional maturity. That is a measure of our real power. It mirrors our ability and willingness to be fully responsible and accountable for everything we say and do, including our attitudes.

Growing in emotional maturity is about becoming more consciously aware of and taking personal responsibility for the choices we make and the impact those choices have. It is about understanding how we unnecessarily continue to restrict ourselves and how, by choice, we can face and end those limitations. It is about increasing recognition, acceptance, and ownership of what we deny or reject about ourselves and our behavior. It is about being willing and able to responsibly be present and deal with what is.

An organization's ability to adapt, innovate and implement change is all significantly impacted by the emotional maturity of its members. How an organization develops its people; its contribution to society, public reputation, profitability, viability, and sustainability; as well as employee attitude, morale and turnover, are all significantly impacted by the emotional maturity and integrity of its members. Economic and political factors, technical expertise, product uniqueness, personal charisma, and the like all have influence and can be important. However they are secondary to the profoundly fundamental impact of emotional maturity and integrity.

As we move from emotional naiveté and immaturity toward being more emotionally intelligent and mature, behaviors manifest that are correspondingly less self-centered, more present, and more honest, authentic, and responsible more of the time. Authentic communication and interpersonal effectiveness dramatically expand, which positively impacts managerial and leadership capabilities as well as personal happiness. That maturation process is sometimes scary and confusing, but, when not hindered or repressed, it is an enormously fulfilling experience and adventure.

6
The Levels of Emotional Maturity

It is not possible for you to influence others to live on a higher level than that on which you live yourself. —Leo Buscaglia

How individuals deal with change and their effectiveness in contributing to themselves, their loved ones, an organization, or to society directly relates to their emotional state and emotional maturity. Although integrity is not highlighted in this chapter, keep in mind that integrity and emotional maturity are inextricably intertwined. Integrity and all its qualities are the essence of emotional maturity.

In reviewing the range of emotions, from positive, loving, contributing, and happy to negative, unloving, selfish, and depressed, we can observe six fairly distinct behavioral levels, each composed of a number of discrete emotions. Each level represents a different attitude or way of perceiving and responding or reacting to life situations. We refer to them as "the levels of emotional maturity":

- **Level 6 — Leader**
- **Level 5 — Doer**
- **Level 4 — Coper**
- **Level 3 — Opposer**
- **Level 2 — Manipulator**
- **Level 1 — Victim**

DIFFERENT PERCEPTIONS CREATE DIFFERENT REALITIES

"Reality" is what we perceive it to be. What that perception is depends on our values, beliefs and attitudes. How we interpret these depends on our emotional state at the time. Our emotions act as filters through which we interpret and respond or react. Attitudes change with each level. Beliefs do also. However, basic values do not change. The values remain the same, but as the filters (emotions) through which they are viewed change, so does the perception and interpretation of their meaning. Each level has its own set of filters that influence how we think and feel and what we decide and choose. Because of the different filters, individuals perceive things differently at different emotional levels. Correspondingly, though the specifics vary, individuals at the same emotional level will tend to have generally similar perceptions of the world around them. They will likely experience the world in quite similar ways. Knowing the characteristics of each level provides us invaluable information in understanding and predicting behavior.

True empowerment, with all its positive aspects, only barely begins at Level 4 and increases exponentially as one moves up the levels (see Figure 6.1, page 142). The higher the level, the greater the fundamental sense of security. This corresponds to a positive willingness and ability to create - to learn, grow and contribute. The higher the level, the greater a person's ability to deal with change constructively. Conversely, at the lower levels, individuals predictably are overwhelmed and dysfunctional in the face of change. The farther down the levels a person is, the more they perceive life situations as problematic.

Although the expression of each level always has cultural and personality nuances and variations, the emotions and emotional levels themselves retain their relationships to each other and their underlying messages. This emotional hierarchy applies to all human beings, regardless of culture, gender or personality differences.

DOING WHAT'S RIGHT—FINDING AN OBJECTIVE MEASURE

What is the "right" thing? By whose standard? Whose interpretation? From what perspective?

Judgments of right or wrong, good or bad, ugly or beautiful are subjective. They are opinions, not facts. At each emotional level, individuals have different subjective but predictable sets of values, beliefs, and associated attitudes and behaviors. By knowing these sets, we can assess the level of emotional maturity. Conversely, by knowing the emotional level at which the person is functioning, we can reliably describe that person's basic attitudes and perspective as well as predict likely behavior.

At any level, individuals are able to provide arguments as to the rightness of their perspectives. How persuasive they are depends on how closely those arguments align with or resonate with those of their audience, which, in turn, depends on the audience's emotional level.

The levels of emotional maturity represent how much essence qualities and values are being actualized. Those qualities, mentioned in chapter 3, are love, authenticity, allowance, forgiveness, presence, generosity, empathy, and integrity, among others. The degree to which these qualities are allowed, encouraged, appreciated, honored, supported, and actually present is a measure of that person's or that organization's emotional maturity.

The more these essence qualities are present, the higher the level of emotional maturity. The higher the level, the broader and more inclusive the viewpoint, the greater the discernment, the less the influence of biases, and the more objective and trustworthy any result-ant evaluation is likely to be. **Therefore, understanding the levels of emotional maturity provides a vehicle to evaluate objectively a person's actual and potential likelihood for both knowing what's right and doing it.**

FIGURE 6.1
Levels of Emotional Maturity and Net Impact
on Self and Others

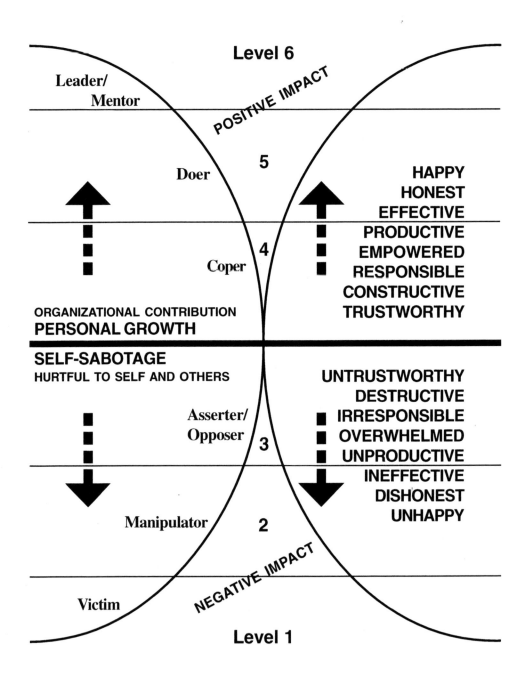

THE SIX LEVELS OF EMOTIONAL MATURITY

Level 6 represents the essence of emotional maturity. At this level, an individual communicates and performs with integrity. Levels 5 through 1 reflect varying degrees of emotional immaturity and a corresponding lack of integrity, with Level 5 being the least immature. As we move down the levels, manifestations of responsible, mature behavior exponentially decline. Below Level 1 is the arena of psychosis (extreme emotional dysfunction). Be cognizant that each level has a range within itself. As we move higher or lower within a level, we begin to see more characteristics common to the next higher or lower level.

Being a good leader is inseparable from being emotionally mature. Effective leaders and responsible associates function at Level 6 or at a high Level 5. These individuals, with their comparatively broad perspective, are aware of and sensitive to others and to different viewpoints. They have an expanded awareness that everything they do has an impact, and that they are responsible and accountable for that impact. For the marginal contributor functioning at Level 4, this sense of responsibility and accountability is rapidly diminishing. For people chronically functioning at Level 3 and below, responsibility is not part of their repertoire, only pretenses of it. These people are dysfunctional and a liability to themselves and others.

Preceding the following descriptions of each of the six levels is a set of Haiku verses. Haiku is a major form of Japanese verse written in 17 [5-7-5] syllables, employing evocative allusions or comparisons. The verses are intended to provide a sense of the flavor that characterizes each level.

LEVEL 6—LEADER

To help others grow
A passionate delight as
Others stretch their might

Strategic thinker
Great presence that sees the
best
That mankind can be

Despite resistance,
As leader he breaks new ground
Courageous is he

He thinks, feels, loves
He balances life forces
Honors you and me

She is a winner
Respects human dignity
Has integrity!

Integrity—yes!
Presence and respect galore!
What more could one ask?

The qualities of integrity are what define this level. At Level 6, individuals live and demonstrate emotional maturity and integrity and, therefore, have a positive, expansive effect on their environment. They know and are secure in their values and thus have a strong sense of self-respect and self-confidence.

Because Leaders respect themselves, they respect the dignity of others. Their self-confidence allows them to candidly confront their limitations and problems and learn from them. They will confront and communicate concerns that their more timid associates tend to couch in social niceties and political correctness. This willingness and ability to face what needs confronting establishes and confirms their maturity. As a result, Leaders have the ability to see the big picture without losing sight of the current picture. They have a wisdom that goes beyond logic and reason without losing sight of logic and reason.

This is often called intuition, and Leaders are willing to act upon it. They have a great sense of personal certainty (not arrogance, subtle or overt, which is a defensive manifestation of Level 2 or Level 3). They are able to make quick, solid decisions. This ability sometimes befuddles their more conservative associates, who are more dependent on external factors and are less willing to honor their intuitive, inner knowing.

In a world unaccustomed to candor, Leaders' forthright, honest communication and authenticity are refreshing to some people but can be uncomfortable for others. Regardless, their authenticity establishes credibility and trust. In fact, natural authentic presence is one of the Leaders most immediately noticeable qualities. When Leaders are with you, they're totally with you—present and attentive. That presence helps them create a trusting space, establish rapport, evaluate priorities, make objective decisions, gain support, ensure quality and timely execution, and manifest constructive results easily.

Leaders are responsible and compassionate mentors. They are ethical motivators who consistently deliver what they promise. In their own unique way, they are responsibly proactive. Whatever the social demeanor or human foibles of Leaders, honesty, authenticity and integrity are at their core. Their social styles may vary widely, from blunt to diplomatic, from "out there" to subdued, but Leaders consciously do the best job they can with the resources they have, to make the world a better place.

Leaders have a predisposition and drive for excellence but are not caught in insatiable demands for perfection. They seek and honestly consider differing viewpoints. They demonstrate, demand, and reward authenticity and responsibility as well as high performance. Compassionate and caring to their core, these people are empowered and will not tolerate or ignore irresponsibility for any reason, including political expedience.

Level 6 is where the ideal win-win relationship has the greatest chance of occurring. This integral environment is the residence of the emotionally wise leader referred to in Chapter 2.

LEVEL 5—DOER

Progressive we are	**We can follow through**
But let's check it out before	**We do strive for excellence**
Starting something new	**Sometimes falling short**
Good people we are	**Able manager**
Still, we have some fears to face	**But to be a great leader,**
To attain greatness	**More boldness needed**

Doers have many of the positive qualities and characteristics of Leaders. They are generally responsible and conscientious. However, they do not quite have the full sense of "I am enough" that characterizes Leaders. As a result, they're still relatively insecure, narrower in perspective, and more influenced by outside social and political pressures and standards. In a sense, they're still trying to "make it." Social image concerns, therefore, are still disproportionately important.

Doers tend to be more conservative than the relatively expansive, proactive people of Level 6. Doers are open to positive ideas, provided the actions or changes do not upset what has been shown to be workable. They are interested enough in positive ideas to check them out. Though they are progressive and will move forward, they like things substantiated first. Once enough data and documentation are provided, they will make a decision. If the decision is positive, they will tend to want to pilot the idea first before committing further. But don't let these conservative approaches belie the fact that these people are emotionally mature enough to be the main producer group in current society.

By contemporary standards, the attitudes and behaviors of individuals functioning on Level 5 are above average. Nevertheless, these people show some signs of emotional immaturity. Consequently, they still manifest less of their potential than they are capable.

LEVEL 4—COPER

First priority—
To find the easiest way
To do the least work

Least effort, their goal
To keep their job, they just do
Enough to get by

Make their life easy
But don't expect a return
They can't be bothered

Contentment is nice
But if stuck too long, it may
Be complacency

They observe and wait
Action is too much bother,
So they do little

Vacant they can be
Shallow they too often are
Much more depth needed

Copers are just responsible and motivated enough to do those things necessary to keep their job but not much more. They want life to be "easy," so they expend as little effort as possible into anything, including growth. They tend to be observers rather than participants. Their attention and interest are mainly on making life easier for themselves. Although not particularly dependable, they are generally likable because they try to avoid disagreements and do little to upset the status quo.

Copers are often described as being mellow. They are likely to be somewhat nonchalant about details and commitments. At level 4, few things are given "big deal" status. Being only marginally responsible, they simply go along. To them, life seems okay, not particularly good but not particularly bad either, just okay. However, unless Copers move toward growth, their contentment will turn to complacency and eventually to contraction. If life is not "comfortable enough," Copers can easily drop into the antagonism of Level 3 and become testy. Copers need to realize this and energize themselves into more proactive behavior.

People functioning at Levels 5 and 6 are assets to an organization or group. Copers, however, are marginal employees. Unless they are willing and able to grow, Copers will only be marginally responsible. Promoting them to positions of responsibility because of seniority or for political reasons will likely create additional management problems. However, sometimes the increased responsibility helps inspire Copers into being more responsible. It will do so rather quickly or not at all. If the latter, the increased responsibility will tend to be overwhelming for the Coper, and lead to lower-level behavior.

BEHAVIOR BELOW LEVEL 4

Between Level 3 and Level 4 is an important dividing line. Above that line, individuals are more secure than insecure and become increasingly more secure as they move up the levels. Below that line, the opposite is true. People operating on the lower three levels have a sense of being overwhelmed by their environment and are insecure and afraid.

The greater the sense of being overwhelmed, the more self-centered, and unhappy people are, regardless of social appearance. Their perspective is narrower and their decisions and actions are correspondingly more irresponsible, defensive, and ineffective. Their behaviors are a reaction to fear and a mask to hide it. Their sense of self-worth, regardless of their social façade, is low. They are reacting in a very limited way to deal with what they perceive as a threat to their survival and even to their very existence. Unfortunately, their reactive behavior is inevitably negative and destructive to themselves and others.

Individuals who are functioning on the lower levels have lost sight of their inherent strengths and power. Their attention is on their weaknesses and limitations. They feel powerless and out of control. They view the world as being hostile and unloving. Their perspective of what is possible is severely limited. They lash out in attempts to regain some semblance of control. Because they feel powerless, they need others also to feel powerless. This arrangement is the only way they feel they can regain some of the control they feel they are losing. They attempt to achieve control through some form of intimidation (Level 3), covert manipulation (Level 2), or appeasement (Level 1). The lower an individual is on the emotional levels, the more likely he is to deceive himself as well as others.

When people function on the lower levels, they do not conform to high-level rules of justice and fair behavior. They may pretend to do so but only because they feel it will give them some manipulative advantage. People operating at more responsible levels sometimes do not understand this and, will attempt to be "reasonable" about putting up with someone's destructive behavior. The higher-level individuals tolerate it because, from their point of view, that sort of irrational behavior does not make sense. Therefore, they assume others "can't be as bad as all that," or should be "given the benefit of the doubt." This approach simply does not work when people are consistently operating on the lower levels. Rather, this "reasonable behavior" is regarded by people operating on the lower levels as foolishly naive, and they will try to take advantage of it.

Individuals operating below Level 4, acutely or chronically, are a liability both to themselves and to their environment. As their sense of feeling overwhelmed increases, their outlook, attitudes, and behavior become increasingly negative. Too often, organizations tolerate low-level behavior rationalizing, "He is so good at doing his main task that we can't afford to lose him." That kind of justification often covers an unwillingness or inability to confront and deal with dysfunctional behavior. It is one of the costliest yet most common errors made in dealing with lower-level individuals or organizations.

Lower level individuals drain energy from everyone around them. They stifle the development of responsibility, creativity, innovation, and morale. Retaining people who chronically function at Level 3 and below, depresses the entire environment. Supervisors who do not correct this behavior or terminate those individuals are failing in their responsibilities. Recognizing and ending the pattern of chronic lower-level behavior is essential to effective leadership and organizational success. It is essential to the development of an emotionally mature environment.

LEVEL 3—OPPOSER

Antagonism—
A sure sign of overwhelm
Testy they sure are

To regain control
They threaten to use such force
To make you give in

Stomp, rage, and bluster
Intimidation their way
To grab your power

Anger they do show—
Under the hostility
Powerless they feel

Level 3 is the first level at which an individual's net impact is more destructive than constructive, both to himself and to his environment. Opposers' certainty and security have gone from positive to negative. Individuals at this level are starting to feel overwhelmed by their environment. As pressures mount, increasingly, the environment is viewed as a threat. Their defense is to lash out, to attack, or to oppose whomever or whatever they perceive to be the problem. This behavior ranges from being testy about specific things to being outright bullies about everything.

Opposers' basic operating mode is to oppose or attack other viewpoints. They do so to compensate for their sense of feeling powerless and out of control. They will exaggerate some element of truth to divert the attention of others from their goals and strengths onto their weaknesses. By intimidating others into fear or apathy, they gain a false sense of control and power. Emotionally, Opposers are either antagonistic or angry. They are often effective at using these to intimidate others into making concessions. If others buy into the intimidation, the Opposers have won. It is important to recognize that intimidating or invalidating behavior only has power when the receiving party goes into agreement with some aspect of the threat or put-down.

For Copers (Level 4), honoring truth and agreements is a casual affair, dependent on what is convenient. Much more forceful, Opposers (Level 3) attack agreements and exaggerate the facts and circumstances to their advantage. As the level of emotional maturity declines, individuals accept less and less responsibility for their actions and increasingly blame others for suboptimal situations or results. Responsibility for one's own actions rapidly disappears and in its place is blame: it is the other person's fault.

In the upper range of Level 3, Opposers display overt hostility and focused opposition. They feel the environment is hostile to their survival, but they think they have some idea who or what is doing them wrong. They resort to antagonistic types of statements such as, "Bookkeeping messed up my account four times!" or "Betty Sue has made errors three times!" The Opposer's focused attacks are based on some exaggerated grievance and blindness to his or her part in creating the situation.

In the lower range of this level, an individual's hostility moves from focused and specific to dispersed and generalized. At the generalized anger level, the antagonistic statement, "Bookkeeping messed up my account four times!" becomes "The organization is always screwing up!" or "They never do it right." "Always," "never," and "they" are often heard in the angry Opposer's statements, such as, "You always do that to me!" or "They never give me the benefit of the doubt!"

However, the social unacceptability of overt hostility can get them fired. As a defense, often they repress the overt expression of hostility. With that repression, the individual deteriorates to Level 2, the Manipulator. The hostility is still present. Only now, it is hidden. The skewing of truth and decreased ability to communicate honestly and productively gets progressively worse as we move down the levels.

LEVEL 2—MANIPULATOR

Deniers of fault	**Deception they do**
Masters of misdirection	**With lies and put-downs**
Stealers of credit	**their tools**
	To cover their fears
Great heights they do want—	**Void of compassion**
Never a concern for whom	**Not loyal or trustworthy**
They often do hurt	**A friend they are not**
By subtle deceits,	**Vicious they sure are!**
Riding the backs of others	**Those who ignore this warning**
Great heights they may gain	**Will pay a big price**

Manipulators are hostile and insecure. They are afraid to express openly their fears and hostility. Rather, they rely on subtle put-downs, misdirection, denials, invalidations, and skillful lying. They hide their hostility and destructive intention with artful deceit and covert manipulation. Individuals at this level are very dangerous. Their underlying hostility is vicious and directed outward. They are expert at hiding their true intentions and, thus, they are difficult to identify and deal with. Individuals at all the other levels are relatively overt in their behaviors and, once you understand their characteristics, are comparatively easy to observe. Not so with this level.

Manipulators have no sense of responsibility—only pretenses of it. They can appear to be socially graceful, real charmers. They are the masters of deception. They can rise to high levels in organizations, usually by subtly manipulating their way into receiving undeserved credit and skillfully misdirecting the blame for their irresponsibility onto others.

Manipulators need to win at any cost. Their purpose is to get others to doubt their own abilities so they can gain some advantage. Their intention is to manipulate others to focus on their weaknesses. They do so by the skillful use of partial truths, subtle put-downs, and invalidations. Manipulators ultimately want others to drop into fear or apathy— to believe that if they do not concede to what the Manipulator wants, the consequences will be even worse.

Manipulators have little concept of exchange or sense of fairness. **Mutual benefit is not their intention. No matter how much they may talk win-win, that talk is only a manipulative ploy.** They regard others as their enemies, and thereby justify any means necessary to "do others in." Their self-centered attitude is that they are only doing what they need to do to survive in this, to them, obviously hostile world.

At this level, the use of manipulation may be quite sophisticated. Manipulators often are able to assume any social level that will meet their hostile and unscrupulous ends. This is the level of the con man, whose intent is to exploit others but not give them the slightest hint of what is actually happening until its too late. They view people who act with compassion, honesty and integrity as simpletons who deserve to be taken advantage of. Using charm and fine manners, they convince Grandma to invest her life savings in a nonexistent venture. They justify such acts as giving trusting people a much-needed learning experience in how the "real world operates."

Although Manipulators can appear charming, sincere, and sophisticated, their actual perception and understanding is quite limited. They are seldom aware enough to realize or acknowledge how destructive their behavior is to themselves, much less to others. What can appear to be intelligent, compassionate behavior is not that at all. Do not confuse intelligence with shrewd manipulation. The "shrewdness" observed at this level is based in fear, entirely self-centered and always limiting and hurtful. That behavior is neither intelligent nor compassionate. The Manipulator's social façade will seldom give even a hint that they are, in fact, very insecure, frightened individuals.

Manipulators identify with the hostility of the Opposer, but are afraid to express it. They silently admire the bravery exhibited by Level 3 Opposer behavior (that is, the willingness to express hostility overtly). This is why displays of strength and willingness to use overt force have an influencing and persuasive effect on people in this level.

Manipulators are compulsive liars and invariably do not deliver what they promise (none of the lower levels do). They tend to have well-justified excuses as to why the important report was late, why they could not keep the meeting, why the something-that-went-wrong was someone else's responsibility. Manipulators do not assume responsibility but instead point fingers. Everything will always appear to have its justifications, including the Manipulator's subtle put-downs. Feeling angry with some situation but having difficulty pinpointing exactly what that is is often an indication of the presence of passive-aggressive behavior.

Don't think there are no crocodiles because the water is calm.

—Mayan proverb

LEVEL 1—VICTIM

I'm just a victim
Of unfair circumstances
Innocent of fault

Overwhelmed I am
What possibly can I do
But whine or appease

One way to control
Be a pathetic victim
To get what I want

Make others guilty
For my life's poor condition—
Suckers they sure are

Victims have an overwhelming sense of powerlessness. The Victim-level individual feels he or she is "about to lose" or "already has lost." Victims believe that the environment has done them in. They have little, if any, sense of responsibility for anything, and truth has little meaning. Victims have a very narrow, self-centered, and selfish viewpoint. They cry, whine, or attempt to appease. Emotional states include self-pity, grief, despair, hopelessness and apathy.

Victims may try to gain some feeble semblance of control by getting others to feel sympathetic toward them. They are experts at creating a very sad story. They attempt to make others feel guilty and uncaring if they do not buy into their victim condition. No matter how much you give or try to help Victims, it is never enough. Eventually, they will accuse and blame you for at least some of their woes. Another form a Victim-level person's behavior may take is in constantly giving, not out of caring or exchange, but as attempts to "buy off" or appease their imagined oppressor. One form of Victim is the yes-man.

Victims' attitudes tend to take some form of, "What's the use? Why bother? I'll never get out of this mess," or "Poor me, look at what they've done to me." Victims will, subtly or otherwise, always let you know they are somehow suffering and that none of their struggle is their responsibility—it's always someone else's fault.

At Level 1, an individual has little, if any, sense of having impact but rather a sense of being affected by everything. Victims do not see solutions, only problems. People who chronically function at the victim level always will have "unsolvable" problems. If offered a solution, Victims will have myriad excuses for how the solution cannot or will not work. In fact, Victims often get upset with people who solve their problems. Since they only know how to operate when their world is full of problems, solving their problems takes away the little sense of control they have and makes them feel more confused.

Victims are usually a problem for only a relatively short period of time, because their general ineffectiveness and crybaby behavior is not tolerated for long, except in codependent situations. This codependency is usually most obvious in family situations and businesses.

ABOUT TEAM BUILDING

Two fundamental ingredients are required to create a true team: (1) honest, open communication, and (2) a common, aligned purpose. The higher the level of emotional maturity and integrity present within an organization, the more likely these fundamentals will be present or created and the easier the process of team building will be. In order to achieve its potential, any true team-building effort must strive to develop both cooperation (involvement with the other to enhance the self) and collaboration (involvement that considers the other's enhancement). It is only with collaboration present that optimum synergy can be attained.

True team building and its synergistic benefits only occur at Levels 5 and 6. Because true collaboration only occurs at Level 6 and high Level 5, team-building attempts at any other level will be predictably ineffective.

Results of cooperation at Level 4 will be marginal and usually short-lived. Cooperation below Level 4 will be a sham. The underlying sense of overwhelm and feelings of hostility of people functioning below Level 4 invariably creates separation and sabotaging behavior. Thus, "cooperative" efforts at these lower levels are, at minimum, a waste of time and ultimately destructive. When individuals operating at the lower levels (lack of integrity) get together, they may generate personal gain, but it inevitably will be at a greater cost to the environment.

Doing one's best to ensure that organizational members are emotionally mature people of integrity is the easiest, most effective and efficient way to vitalize an organization. Doing so enhances individual and team development, increases performance, raises morale, and expands profitability.

The levels of emotional maturity correspond closely with the motivational models presented earlier. In comparing them, (see Table 6.1) we observe that at the highest level of emotional maturity, an adult has a well-developed, mature ego, experiences inclusive self-actualization, and is motivated by growth and responsible action. As we move into the lower emotional levels, we observe an increasingly self-centered and problematic narrowing of focus.

TABLE 6.1
Correlation of the Levels of Emotional Maturity
with Three Models of Motivation

Levels of Emotional Maturity	Stages of Ego Development	Maslow's Hierarachy of Needs	Herzberg's Two-Factor Job Model
Leader	Mature Adult "I am enough."	Self-Actualization	Motivational Factors Growth Potential Responsibility
Doer	Adolescent/ Young Adult "Am I learning, doing, growing, being enough?"	Esteem	Achievement Recognition Advancement
Coper		Belonging	Maintenance Factors Interpersonal Relations— Peers,
Opposer	Child/Young Adolescent "Am I good enough?"		Supervisors, Subordinates
		Security	Company Policy
Manipulator			Job Security
	Infant/Young Child "Am I getting enough?		Work Conditions
Victim		Survival	Salary

The following table (Table 6.2) presents a variety of attitudinal and behavioral characteristics for each level. It has proven useful in: (1) assessing an individual's (or group's) emotional level, (2) anticipating behaviors not yet observed, and (3) determining the kind of communication most likely to facilitate movement up the levels.

TABLE 6.2 - The Levels Of Emotional Maturity, Immaturity— Corresponding Characteristics And Behaviors

		A Chronic Patterns	B Emotional Stability/ Orientation	C Associated Emotions/ Attitudes
Level 6 **Leader**	Emotional Maturity	High integrity. Comfortable presence. Clear focus. Big picture. Considerate of real needs. Positive action and results. Appreciates and enjoys life. Life is an adventure. Humor.	High emotional stability. Very sane. Expresses and deals with entire range of emotions easily. High emotional resiliency.	Passionate. Enthusiastic. Happy, joyful. Strong interest.
Level 5 **Doer**		Conscientious. Positive "provided" claims are substantiated. "Pleasant."	Generally stable. Reasonably sane. Can express and deal with most of the emotional range. Fair to good emotional resiliency.	Positive/progressive. Open, interested.
Level 4 **Coper**		More an observer than a participant. Casual, "mellow." Takes the path of least resistance. Careless.	Marginal stability. Restricted emotional range. Can easily become irritable under minimal stress.	Contentment. Neutral. Disinterest.
Level 3 **Opposer**	Emotional Immaturity	Sees world as hostile, threatening. Narrow emotional range. Best defense is an offense. "Angry person." "The debater."	Unstable. Hostile outbursts. Criticizes, blames, threatens, intimidates.	Irritable. Antagonistic. Overt anger. Resentment.
Level 2 **Manipu-lator**		World is so threatening that must hide own fear, hostile intentions and behaviors. Highly Self-absorbed. "The con man." "The gossip." "The martyr." "The two-face."	IPretends emotional stability not in fact present. Uses manipulative, subtle invalidations. Often pretends to be operating at Level 5 or 6.	Unexpressed resentment. Unsympathetic. Passive-Aggressive. Covert hostility. Fear. Anxiety.
Level 1 **Victim**		Cry baby. Complainer. Whiner or just "numbed out." "Poor me." "Yes man." "The victim."	Minimal emotional stability or resiliency. "Can't do anything about it." Emotional basket case.	Regret. Self-pity. Grief. Despair. Hopeless. Apathy. Numb.

D Productivity/ Ability To Execute	**E** Learning Capacity	**F** Interest		
Highly productive.Gets positive results fast, effortlessly. Completes cycles of action. Can-do attitude. Excellent follow-through.	Open to new concepts. Evaluation & discernment skills finely tuned. High ability to differentiate relative importances. Quick study.	Broad, far-reaching interests. High sense of the aesthetics of life, people, things. Gets involved with focus and intensity. High enjoyment of many things/ activities. Life is an opportunity. Passionate about life.	Willing / Can Do	**Level 6**
Usually productive. "Will try to do it" attitude. Completes most things.	Open to concepts supported by experience. Fair to good differentiation abilities.	Narrower scope of interests than Level 6. Enjoys/ participates in/ focuses on a relatively limited number of things.		**Level 5**
Marginal. Will do just enough to get by. Many things left incomplete.	Indifferent. Marginal student.	Neutral about most things. Casual, detached observer rather than a participant. Interested in things that make his/her life easier.	Pretended Willingness / Unwilling / "Can't Do"	**Level 4**
Destructive. Will oppose real productivity. "Executes" by the use of force/threat. Short-term "results" only. Burns out subordinates.	Rejects new concepts as threatening.	Interested in opposing, attacking, and aggressive defence.		**Level 3**
"Apparently" productive, but actually highly destructive. Will covertly undermine real productivity and positive results. Often "sophisticated" excuses.	Pretends openness to new concepts, but is threatened by them so covertly invalidates them.	Fascinated by things and tricks that can be used to manipulate or put down others for selfish interests.		**Level 2**
Zero.	Non-existent. "It's impossible, why bother." Can't do attitude.	No real interest in actions or activities outside of themselves. Attention solely on problems for which they refuse to take action or responsibility. Totally self-absorbed.		**Level 1**

		G Trustworthy	H Handling Of Truth	I Willingness To Confront
Level 6 **Leader**	Honest / Authentic	Definitely!	Bluntly truthful to self and constructively truthful with others. Honesty, authenticity, forthrightness, hallmarks.	Will confront whatever needs to be dealt with. Observational abilities finely tuned. Willingness to explore other beliefs and to reassess one's own. Great presence.
Level 5 **Doer**		Most of the time.	Reasonably truthful to self and socially truthful to others.	Selective confront. Fair to good observational abilities. Cautious progress.
Level 4 **Coper**	↓	Marginal.	Casual about truth. Careless of facts. Insincere.	Minimal confront. Observational skills minimal. Difficult situations are avoided or ignored.
Level 3 **Opposer**	Dishonest / Pretense / Deceit	No.	Predictably exaggerates negative aspects. Blames others. Angry when own exaggerations/negative impact noted.	Attacks others to avoid confronting own irresponsibility. Tends to back down quickly when threats do not work.
Level 2 **Manipu-** **lator**		No!!	Chronic, but "artful" liar. Subtly twists the truth to confuse and invalidate others. Uses "truth" to hurt.	Covertly manipulates and misdirects to avoid confronting and owning any responsibility.
Level 1 **Victim**	↓	You must be kidding!	Will say anything to gain sympathy or appease.	Avoids almost all issues. Too inwardly focused to observe much at all.

J Ethics/Integrity	K Responsibility	L Real Sense Of Self-Esteem And Self-Worth		
Truly "walks their talk." Responsibly acts on what he/she believes to be correct action, even if in conflict with social/moral/current norms. Principles and character solid. Has courage to act on convictions.	Outstanding. Willing and able to respond appropriately and joyously. Faces and deals with whatever needs to be confronted.	Fully own their worthiness. Honest, positive self-evaluation. Not dependent on others' opinions for their esteem, only for feedback.	Responsible	Level 6
Reasonable ethics, but is influenced by social and moral standards. "Walks their talk" most of the time.	Acceptable. Attention on maintaining and improving what currently works.	Somewhat more dependent on others for sense of esteem and worthiness.		Level 5
Goes along with social and moral conventions if convenient to do so. Little real integrity. Convenience and "getting by" of senior importance.	Marginal to poor. Will demonstrate responsibility only to maintain position and little more. Careless.	Marginal.		Level 4
Fights social/moral codes as stupid, arcane. "The revolutionary." Attacks those with Integrity and/or those who point out integrity deficiencies.	Irresponsible. Views responsibility as a burden. Overtly blames others. Attacks & accuses to avoid own responsibility.	Low. Masked by arrogant or macho behavior.	Irresponsible / Blame	Level 3
Pretends integrity, but definitely lacking. Facade of "noble" moral platitudes & justifications to the effect that the "ends justify the means." Politically "correct." "The subversive."	"Apparently" responsible, but actually highly irresponsible. Covertly misdirects blame to others. Capricious.	Very low. Masked by "sophisticated" facade, pretense, and lies.		Level 2
Will do anything to fend off the "oppressor." All behaviors for which they are continually "sorry" are "justified" by their victim condition.	Almost totally irresponsible. "It's not my fault."	Non-existent.		Level 1

		M Sense Of Being Able To Handle Life	N Concept Of Fairness And Exchange	O Persistence On A Given Course
Level 6 **Leader**	Rational / Feeling	Definitely! True confidence that they can, at minimum, cope with life's contingencies, no matter what they are.	Outstanding. Gives and demands fair exchange. Strong sense of justice for all concerned. Balanced perspective. Will not tolerate dishonest or unjust behavior.	Strong, creative persistence and direction toward constructive goals. Thorough follow-up. Gets the best results possible under adverse conditions.
Level 5 **Doer**		Generally has sense of being able to handle most	Decent. Generally acceptable.	Fair to good persistence, if obstacles are not too great.
Level 4 **Coper**	Misemotional	Marginal. Limited to making personal life easier, more comfortable.	Expects partners to contribute without much consideration to equal exchange. "Cheap."	Poor persistence and concentration. Will shift focus in face of obstacles or inconvenience.
Level 3 **Opposer**	Feeling / Irrational /	Starting to feel over-whelmed. "Uses" macho behavior as a defensive compensation.	Demands more than worth. Uses threats to get more than otherwise would. Uses blame to avoid what owes.	Destructive persistence. Begins strongly, weakens quickly.
Level 2 **Manipu-** **lator**	Repressed	Feels overwhelmed. "Cool" demeanor covers sense of inadequacy. Too afraid to fight back openly, so does so via covert means.	Does not deliver as promised. No real concept of exchange. Selfish, self-centered. Lies about value provided. "Something for nothing." Creates excuses to avoid fair payment. Criminal.	Vacillation on any given course except to manipu-late others, "get even," or "get something for nothing."
Level 1 **Victim**		Virtually totally overwhelmed. "Can do nothing about it." Victim mentality.	Expects to be taken care of with no exchange.	Sporadic persistence toward self-destruction.

P Goals/Time	**Q** Thought/ Decision Making Process	**R** Handling Of Agreements		
Focused goals. Very much in the present. Creates time to accomplish many things. Action toward expansive future. Willing to delay gratification for greater future benefit.	Highly attuned observational abilities. Broad perspective & positive attitudes provide basis for fast, decisive, highly rational decisions and choices. Respect and empathy fully integrated in decision-making process.	"Delivers what they promise." Will not knowingly violate valid agreements except to meet truly higher ethical imperatives. Does not use the higher imperative as a justification.	Productive/Constructive	**Level 6**
Goals shorter term and smaller scale than Level 6. Reasonable present time focus.	Decisions rational, but perspective compared to Level 6 somewhat narrower, resulting in slower, more complicated, and less sophisticated reasoning.	May justify breaking agreements for practical considerations. May use higher imperative as a justification.		**Level 5**
Unfocused, minimal goals. "Waiting for it to happen." Dispersed, little sense of time.	Barely rational—indecisive. Decisions/ choices are narrow and self-centered.	Often indifferent to agreements. Does what is momentarily convenient.		**Level 4**
No sense of future consequences. Demands instant gratification. Goals are to attack "opposition" now, before it gets worse.	No longer rational or responsible, but opposing. Irresponsible. Destructive decisions and choices.	Openly attacks and fights agreements. Exaggerates and blames others as an excuse.	Unproductive / Destructive	**Level 3**
Goals are to misdirect a hostile worlds attention away from self and "get even" covertly for real or imagined "wrongs" of the past. Subtle, "persuasive reasons" why doesn't deliver as promised.	Almost totally reactive. Real, constructive analytical abilities gone. Choices and decisions destructive for all concerned. Apparent "sophistication" is actually a facade based on lies, manipulations.	Pretends to honor agreements, but always has "justified" reasons for breaking them. Skillful "use" of the legal system for own selfish ends.		**Level 2**
Zero goals except survival. Attention on past. Major regrets. No time to do anything so does nothing.	Irrational, no analytic abilities extant. Decisions, or lack of them, destructive. No sense of having a choice in anything.	Whines about "imposed" agreements that they "couldn't" do anything about.		**Level 1**

		S Relationships	T Handling Of Control/Power
Level 6 **Leader**	Empathetic / Caring	High degree of mutual responsibility and trust. Happy, joyous, co-creative. Long term potential high. Loyalty high. Honors commitments. Vulnerability and real intimacy high. Treats people fairly and with respect.	Very strong sense of being able to positively control all aspects of life. Very secure—helps others empower themselves. Willing to lead or follow as appropriate. Power = ability and willingness to act = ability to get sane, productive effects. Execution and follow-up outstanding.
Level 5 **Doer**		Decent sense of contribution. Satisfied with most relationships. Reasonably happy.	Less of above. Feels generally adequate about controlling most of life's situations. Willing & able to act responsibly & effectively most of the time.
Level 4 **Coper**	Self-absorbed / Self-centered / Selfish / Uncaring	Shallow. Not happy—not unhappy. Casual about commitment. No real intimacy. Multiple short term relationships or stays with one partner because it's a hassle to move.	Follows orders in a slipshod manner. Respects and wants sane direction and focus. Sense of wasting life away, but not knowing how to be in more positive control. Low-level chronic anxiety. Willingness & ability to act diminishing.
Level 3 **Opposer**		Demanding, bully, threatening, macho. Potential sadist. Casual shifts in loyalty for selfish gain. Unhappy. Does not honor commitments, but demands others honor theirs. Fights intimacy. Blames partners for its lack. Creates dependencies.	Starting to feel overwhelmed—out of control. Compensates by lashing out. Feels must control others. Will resent and oppose orders from others. Power = "power over" by overt domination. Disempowers others.
Level 2 **Manipu-** **lator**		Emotionally suppressive. Terrified of real intimacy. Subtle continuous put-downs, make wrongs and invalidations. No real concept of relationship. Creates dependencies. Predictability promiscuous.	Underlying fear of losing all—too afraid to lash out. Compulsive need to control others by manipulation, lies, invalidation, and misdirection—seeks hidden power. Power = "power over" by covert dominion. Disempowers others.
Level 1 **Victim**		Demands to be taken care of. Gross co-dependency. Miserable.	No sense of controlling anything. Feeble attempts to control by getting others to feel guilty or sorry for them—brings others down to their level through pity. Feels powerless Underlying rage.

U — Attitudes Toward Life	V — Form Of Communication	W — Win-Win Outcome		
Views experiences including losses as an opportunity and a challenge to learn and grow. Life is an adventure. Curious about, enjoys life most of the time. "We can."	Authentic. Encourages real dialogue. Will not tolerate destructive, dishonest communications. Excellent listener. Acknowledges well.	Outstanding probability. Even "losses" are a learning experience from which to expand and grow.	Secure / Happy	**Level 6**
Some experiences are opportunities and can be interesting—most are OK. "Life isn't bad."	Reasonable, open to viewpoints that do not stray too far from the status quo. Tolerates "social lies." "Devil's Advocate."	Decent probability.		**Level 5**
"I'm not unhappy." "It's someone else's responsibility." "I can't be bothered."	Casual conversation. Devaluates urgencies. Glib, superficial, mundane.	Possible, but remote.		**Level 4**
Most experiences are threatening. "It's a hostile world." "Must be tough." Angry at most things. Critical of people, situations, and life.	Blames. Attacks. Demands. Opposes or rejects other viewpoints. Sarcastic. Angry or antagonistic. "Debater."	No.	Insecure / Unhappy	**Level 3**
Most experiences are a lie. People out to con you. Better get them before they get you. Cynical.	Uses subtle forms of invalidation as put-downs. Twists, depreciates positive communication. Expert at creat-ing "reasonable" excuses for non-delivery of what is promised. Misleading.	Definitely not! (Don't be fooled by the promises—they're invariably exaggerations and lies.)		**Level 2**
Life is overwhelming. It's sad, or despairing and "there's nothing I can do about it." "I can't."	Expressions of worry, fear, pleas for sympathy, or attempts at appeasement.	Forget it!		**Level 1**

		X Typical Eye Contact	Y Has Rapport With	Z Motivated By
Level 6 **Leader**	Courage	Can look at you directly, comfortably with interest. "Real contact." Communicates presence.	Positive, caring, responsible viewpoints, actions, and results. High Integrity.	Demonstrations of authenticity integrity, compassion and positive action.
Level 5 **Doer**		Less of above.	People, things, and communication that supports, enhances a status quo.	Big picture. Expanded possibilities. Personal growth opportunity. Level 6 behavior.
Level 4 **Coper**		No real eye contact. Casual, indifferent contact. Just as interested in looking at the paperweight as you.	Being entertained. "Laid back" activities. Not being hassled.	Those things that make their job or situation "easier."
Level 3 **Opposer**	Lack Of Courage / Cowardice	Looks at you as a target to attack.	Statements and actions of overt hostility against a perceived common enemy.	"Mellow" behavior. They need to be heard. Will tend to be persuaded by those with patience and the ability to truly listen.
Level 2 **Manipu-** **lator**		Ranges from cold, indifferent stare to "apparent, charming" interest.	Gossip. Covert, subtle, invalidations of others. Cynicism.	Willingness to use overt force against perceived common "threat." Underlying fear causes them to hide their hostility. Will follow those "brave" enough to be overtly hostile.
Level 1 **Victim**		Ranges from fearful fleeting avoidance to inward, unfocused.	Sympathy and agreement with how they've been victimized.	Statements of fear and covert actions against the "enemy."

SUMMARY OF LEVEL BEHAVIOR

Individuals or organizations operating chronically at Levels 1, 2, and 3 are emotionally challenged. They will manifest correspondingly limited viewpoints, attitudes, abilities, and behaviors. At Level 4 this also will be true, but less so. People operating at Levels 4 and above demonstrate increasing responsibility, trustworthiness, and a win-win viewpoint. It is only at sustained Levels 5 and 6 that we find individuals and organizations that are capable of capitalizing on their larger potential.

Individuals and organizations at Levels 1-3 are defensively and reactively hostile to change, no matter how needed. At Level 4, they generally are mildly resistant to change because it is a "bother," unless it is to their personal advantage. At Level 5, they are open to and supportive of responsible change. At Level 6, they proactively encourage and embrace responsible change.

Level 6 Leaders offer the broadest perspective and most consistently responsible, mature behavior. They demonstrate authenticity, rational certainty, and creativity in proactively expanding and balancing relevant factors. They expect, demand, and model integral behavior. These emotionally mature individuals live the qualities that create a sane, healthy environment where win-win situations are, in fact, the norm.

Level 5 Doers are mostly positive and action- and results-oriented, but with a proviso—that their willingness to move, expand, and try new things occur *after* they first thoroughly test, examine, and validate what they're learning along the way. They tend to be proactive devil's advocates.

Level 4 Copers are only slightly more positive than negative and are characterized by doing just enough things right to get by.

Level 3 Opposers and the levels below represent a lose-lose situation in which individuals perceive themselves as being overwhelmed by their environment and so they fight back in the only ways they know how. Level 3 Opposers and those lower on the scale of emotional maturity negatively affect their colleagues and workplace, resulting in compromised honesty, responsibility, and meaningful contributions. At Level 3, individuals are still strong enough to overtly lash out at their environment in the form of opposition, attack, and intimidation, which are emotionally characterized by antagonism and anger. At this level, people are not only obviously hostile but, despite their bluster, frightened.

Level 2 Manipulators are too frightened even to outwardly express their hostility, so they go undercover. They cover their passive aggressive hostility with social niceties, deceits, and subtle invalidations of others that are always destructive but difficult to spot.

Level 1 Victims feel as though they have already lost. The emotions most characterized by people caught in this level are self-pity, grief, despair, hopelessness and apathy. Victim behavior takes on pathetic forms of helplessness to gain sympathy or gross attempts at appeasement.

Points to consider:

- What are some examples of the values, beliefs, attitudes, positions, and behaviors that are typical or likely for each of the six levels of emotional maturity, immaturity?
- At what level do you think your organization operates? List specific attitudes and behaviors.
- At what level do you think you behave most of the time? Take your time on this one. It is our willingness and ability to observe and honestly take responsibility for all aspects of our behavior that is the key to our empowerment, growth and personal sense of fulfillment.

7
The Power of Communication

If you would persuade, you must appeal to interest rather than intellect. —Benjamin Franklin

The ability to accurately assess levels of emotional maturity and facilitate individual movement to higher levels of emotional maturity is foundational to both interpersonal growth and organizational effectiveness. It is a core competency and crucial to leadership and management development.

Helping to facilitate others toward greater emotional maturity requires that the facilitators themselves be emotionally mature. Otherwise, their intentions and actions simply will not be productive. People who function at Level 3 (Opposer; see Chapter 6) or below will be counterproductive. Additionally, a facilitator needs to understand and be able to apply good communication skills, which include recognizing and dealing with repressed communication. When those skills are lacking, facilitating emotional maturity is much more problematic. How an individual or a group communicates, including how they respond or react to communication, is one of the best indicators of that individual or group's level of emotional maturity. Before we deal directly with the dynamics of facilitating people up the levels (addressed in Chapter 8), we'll first briefly review some communication basics and their application, which are too often forgotten or ignored.

GOOD LISTENERS – A RARE COMMODITY

Good listeners are a rather rare commodity in a world of busy people trying to get other busy people's attention. We feel we must "be on," must say the bright thing, make the "great" presentation, and look good no matter what. That emphasis on the need to perform has contributed to repressing our willingness, ability and skill at listening. It has created a culture where slick performances based on glib one-liners rules the day. The emphasis is on performing at the expense of listening. Let's face it, we're not learning very much when we're doing all the talking. There is nothing wrong with talking, or performing, if balanced with appropriate listening and acknowledging.

Rather than putting so much attention on being interesting, it behooves us all to put more emphasis on our ability to listen, to pay real attention to the other person's needs, wants, aspirations, to be interested in them and their perspectives.

We often talk of the importance of establishing rapport but too often forget that one of the most powerful and elegant ways to do so is simply to be a good listener. Good listening, like good acknowledging, communicates interest in the other person. Attentive listening acts as a validation of the other person. This is usually highly appreciated and usually reciprocated. Besides, we learn a lot more when we listen than when we "perform" – and we make far fewer mistakes.

How often do we break rapport by doing things like minimizing what the other person is saying? How often do we interrupt by sharing similar stories, diagnosing, criticizing, rescuing, advising or fixing? We would be far better off talking less, and consciously being more present and attentive, listening with interest, acknowledging as appropriate, and speaking primarily to verify for clarification and understanding. Suggested reading: *Listening Leaders* by Steil and Bommelji.

THE VALUE OF ACKNOWLEDGMENTS

Acknowledgment is one of the most underrated, misunderstood, and underused of the basic communication skills. Most of us continually under-acknowledge, over-acknowledge, or—most commonly—do not bother to acknowledge at all.

How another person is acknowledged has a significant impact on his or her attention to and evaluation of what is communicated, ability to use the data later, and feelings of self-esteem. Understanding what constitutes acknowledgment, as well as its impact, can increase our effectiveness and the esteem in which we are held by others.

An effective acknowledgment communicates to the other person that his or her communication was received and understood. It does not necessarily imply acceptance or rejection, only "Thank you, I understand and appreciate what you said." Proper use of an acknowledgment keeps the speaker from wondering, "Did they get it or didn't they?" It lets the speaker know that he need not repeat. Acknowledgments also validate the other person, because they let him know that the communication was valuable enough for the listener to pay attention and respond to.

Failure to acknowledge even the simplest of communications is one of the most common and devastating errors in day-to-day communication. This leads to more misunderstandings than we can imagine. How many times have you failed to give a simple acknowledgment to a communication that you understood? You probably reasoned that there was no need for acknowledgment, that it was obvious that you got it. But was it? The person trying to communicate with you is not always sure of that. Providing no acknowledgment leaves some doubt, and the other person's attention tends to remain on the communication. As a result, the person may repeat it unnecessarily, which is frustrating to both of you. Another common reaction is that the person feels slighted because she thinks you did not even bother to take the time to say, "I heard you." Whatever affinity there may have been in the beginning can quickly erode, sometimes to the point of a dramatic outburst. You may be baffled and think the other person is a little crazy, or you may be critical of yourself for being ineffective. Most times, neither of those results will occur if you acknowledge the communication.

Some cultures are much more aware of the importance and use of acknowledgments than others are and use them more frequently. This can also lead to misunderstandings.

Americans tend to be poor acknowledgers and are relatively imprecise in their communications. This creates many unnecessary upsets. Lack of acknowledgement has sometimes created huge misunderstandings and, in many instances, spurred negative attitudes that are largely unjustified. For example, an American negotiator says to his Japanese counterpart, "I think you should order X widgets." The Japanese negotiator says, "Hi, domo," which means, "Yes—thanks." The American takes this as an agreement and assumes that he has an order. To the Japanese however, his acknowledgment simply meant "Thank you—I understand that you would like me to order X widgets." The intention is not to indicate acceptance or agreement. It is simply a polite acknowledgment of what the negotiator said.

When the order does not materialize, the American may feel the Japanese negotiator was disingenuous. If that occurs often enough, the American may develop an attitude of, "You just can't trust those people." The Japanese on the other hand may start to wonder how they should deal with those irrational Americans.

Culture is not part of this book's scope. However, it is a significant factor. It is one that anyone dealing with other cultures needs to be acutely aware.

FROM DISCUSSION TO DIALOGUE—MOVING TOWARD GREATER UNDERSTANDING

The primary purpose of communication is to expand understanding. More often, however, "communication" involves one or both parties trying to convince the other of the "rightness" of their viewpoint. There is little, if any, real listening or acknowledgment from either party.

How often do we observe different viewpoints taken as attacks that "need" defending against rather than as simply different viewpoints? Rather than expanding understanding, these "attempts" at "communication" result in upsets, increased intolerance, and diminished understanding. Scientist David Bohm calls this form of counterproductive "communication" **discussion**. He suggests we would be much better served by **dialogue** than by discussion.

In true dialogue, judgments are consciously suspended. There is only the presentation of viewpoints. An opinion is recognized as simply one viewpoint of many possible viewpoints. There are no attempts to convince the other party, defend a position, or obtain specific results. Rather, there is the intention to set aside prejudices, truthfully share viewpoints, and be open and honestly desire to learn about and from the other person's perspective.

The willingness of all parties to learn from each other is a quality of and essential for dialogue. When that willingness is present, dialogue takes place just by being together. When we are truly open and believe there is something valuable to learn from the other party, then we expand awareness, not only of the other person but also of ourselves. Not only does dialogue expand the breadth of understanding, but it also offers the probability of reaching greater depths within ourselves.

For dialogue to be meaningful, **both** parties must be open to the positive and the negative aspects of their respective positions. **Both** parties must understand that there can be truth outside their current set of "truths." **Both** parties need to be open to the possibility that by engaging in dialogue their position and viewpoint might change.

By the act of observing and listening with the intention to learn, we are able to appreciate the beauty and value of other viewpoints as well as our own. In fact, the ability and willingness to be present with another person's perspective opens up many new possibilities.

This is freedom—freedom **from** the limitation of our own self-imposed intolerance and the unconfronted fear that fuels it. It is also freedom *to* learn and grow. With real dialogue, we are more receptive to viewpoints previously rejected out of hand. True dialogue helps us develop empathy. It is validating and honoring to all parties. It increases rapport and builds respect. It broadens our consideration of what is possible. It expands our options and choices.

An unwillingness to dialogue is an indication that fear and some sense of "overwhelm" is at least acutely, if not chronically, present. This must be dealt with before honest communication can take place. If the situation is acute rather than chronic, skillful use of facilitation level (developed in Chapter 8) can often move a person to an emotional state where real dialogue can take place. As long as the sense of overwhelm remains, true dialogue will not be present and the situation will usually not resolve without outside intervention.

True dialogue only occurs at Levels 5 and 6 of the levels of emotional maturity (see Chapter 6, *The Levels of Emotional Maturity*). By recognizing when we are in a discussion rather than a dialogue, we open the door to improving real communication. By owning how we are creating, allowing, or contributing to an unproductive form of interaction, we are taking responsibility for our impact and are thus empowering ourselves. By consciously and proactively changing from discussion to dialogue, we open the door to a whole new world of expanded awareness. True dialogue should be our **conscious intention** in every interaction.

LESSENING REPRESSED COMMUNICATION

Results are the manifestation of our acting with willingness and intention. Real feelings give our willingness and intention "juice." When feelings are repressed, we go "numb" and have no juice. Our intention is weakened and dispersed. Authentic communication is lost. The "results" are always less than of what we are capable. They are accompanied by some sense of disappointment, frustration, inadequacy and, oftentimes, blame.

Chronically repressed communication is always based in fear. It indicates some form of insecurity. This is the primary cause of very little, if any, real communication occurring among groups in the same organization. The degree to which communication is repressed is the degree to which real collaboration and true teamwork are limited. This, in turn, limits innovation, productivity, and profitability.

Lessening, if not eliminating, repressed communication is a crucial aspect of creating true teams and manifesting the synergy true teams are potentially capable of producing. The process of clearing interpersonal communications may have the important added benefit of clarifying and focusing personal values, which, until elucidated, can confuse and confound organizational values.

When repressed communication is released, an amazing phenomenon occurs. A seemingly disproportionate amount of positive energy comes forth, and a willingness to be open and vulnerable spontaneously occurs. Individuals become more allowing, tolerant, and open to new viewpoints. Rapport increases, along with a willingness to trust and to share thoughts and ideas, even if those ideas are "far out."

That **willingness** to candidly share is one of the two fundamental elements of a true team. The other element that develops a potential team into an actual team is a **mutual focus** that each member feels ownership in and a commitment to. Without candid communication, attention is dispersed and mutual focus is much harder to achieve. With repressed communication present, there is no true team, only a group of individuals.

Handling repressed communication also generates a significantly greater willingness and ability on our part to look at and own previously unconscious, but nonetheless self-imposed and thus self-limiting, considerations.

What does it take to end repression? Organizationally, it takes a leadership committed to creating a safe, secure environment where one is free to express their opinions, needs and desires. Individually, it takes courage to face the fear of letting go of old, familiar, comfortable but dysfunctional patterns. It takes commitment to persist through the inevitable resistance to any change—our own and that of others—and it takes willingness to communicate honestly and respectfully.

In many cultures, indirectness and social "politeness" are expected norms of "proper" behavior. In those cultures, candor is often resisted—sometimes strongly—and always rationalized. These norms should not be arrogantly ignored but, rather, appreciated for their original intention of respecting individual human dignity. However, far too often the original intention has been lost and has deteriorated into little more than a "justification" for lack of honesty, candor, and authenticity, which, in turn, is a cover to avoid acknowledging, facing, and feeling underlying fears of inadequacy.

Honestly assessing what is respect for and what is fear of honest expression must be done conscientiously and responsibly. Social norms should be considered and, as appropriate, appreciated and honored, but **never** at the expense of honesty. Ultimately, lack of honesty is **always** based in fear, no matter how rationalized.

The following plan is a method for lifting repressed communication:

1. Require candor and honesty as a fundamental condition of continued employment. (Note how many people, directly or indirectly, regard this requirement as ridiculously impractical—a rather telling indication of the actual level of communication and inefficiencies present.) This may be scary for some people, and for those who are afraid, this requirement just brings the fear that was already there to the surface;

2. Initiate programs that clarify and provide an understanding of what real communication and emotional maturity are, how they manifest, and what individuals need to do to grow and expand;

3. Offer competent, confidential, one-on-one coaching to help selected individuals uncover or express what they have repressed. This coaching is highly personal and tailored to the individual. Ensure the coaches can competently apply the facilitation skills presented in Chapter 8. (Also, see *In-Depth Probing to Determine Real Needs, Concerns, and Values,* this Chapter, page 178, and *The Value of Competent Coaching,* Chapter 8, page 205.);

4. Offer confidential, competently facilitated, small-group sessions in which individuals can feel safe to express themselves and, as appropriate, clear "upsets" or confusion with group members. The intention is to use the group process to help individuals develop the willingness and skills to communicate from a basis of authenticity. An important aspect is to help the participants gain clarity about their own needs. Immature, insecure people often will use these activities as "opportunities" to "dump" on others. Therefore, competent facilitation is necessary;

5. Implement the above steps with enough people and reinforcement to attain critical mass.

The higher the emotional maturity of individuals and an organization, the less repressed the communication that will be present. Imagine for a moment what your family, group, or organization would be like and how the world would feel if everyone felt safe enough to be authentic in his or her communication.

FOCUS OF ATTENTION

The truly great performers, presenters, and communicators have two things in common: First, they are professionals and know their material. Second, and even more important, they are in excellent communication with their audience; that is, they have their attention on their audience, not on themselves. Their intention is to deliver something of value to someone. The more a person is interested in us, the more we become interested in him or her.

Good communicators keep their interest, attention, and intention on their audience, not on themselves. To the degree we can do this, not only will we be more effective and interesting to our audience (whether one person or 500 people), but we will also find that the entire process of communicating is much less of an effort. We will communicate greater naturalness, poise, and presence. We will be less nervous and have more fun.

IN-DEPTH PROBING TO DETERMINE REAL NEEDS, CONCERNS AND VALUES

This section on probing utilizes a sales context as an example. However, the principles and dynamics are applicable to any interpersonal interaction. They are particularly useful where the intention is to go deeper in discovering underlying needs and intentions. Graciously applied, in depth probing is useful in any communication situation It is especially valuable in a therapeutic setting.

Sales pros know that people buy benefits, not features. This is true, but which benefits? Individuals differ considerably in what they value. While there is some overlap in human motivation, people have unique needs, wants, and aspirations, some of which change as circumstances change. Many a sale has been lost because the needed benefit was not offered or the "inappropriate" one was presented. To discover the benefit or benefits that meet your prospect's unique needs, **in-depth probing** can be very useful. The probing should be "in-depth" for two reasons:

1.   The prospect is often not aware of exactly what she needs or wants;

2. It may not occur to the prospect to tell you a particular need because she has no idea that you could or would be willing to meet it.

Successful in in-depth probing is dependent on the following:
*   Your being "present";
*   Your genuine willingness to listen and understand the other person's unique needs and point of view;
*   Your competence in applying in-depth probing, without becoming rote.

In-depth probing is a highly individualized process and cannot be conducted in a rote fashion. Good rapport must be established. Understanding and initially matching the other person's emotional level is key.

Engendering confidence by really "being there" with the other person and taking a sincere interest in him or her is an essential part of the in-depth probing process. Your ability to comfortably maintain presence, listen willingly, and acknowledge effectively will do more toward selling you and your product than anything else. Technical competence, impressive credentials, and a professional can all be very helpful. Those attributes should not be slighted, but they are of secondary importance to the in-depth probing process.

Remember, you are the purveyor of your product. If people don't buy you, they usually are much less willing to buy what you are selling. They are much less likely to buy you if you are not sincerely interested in them and willing to listen to their needs, wants and aspirations. There are two types of probing questions that can be used to obtain important data about your prospect's needs.

Types of Probing Questions

1. The Directive Question. The directive question is specific and focused. Questions that can be answered with a simple yes or those that can be addressed with short, specific answers tend to be directive questions. Examples of such questions are: Who? What? Where? How much? How many? Which of the two? They may be appropriate for obtaining specific information, but usually are not conducive to establishing rapport or good two-way communication. Too many directive questions can be perceived as interrogation and break rapport.

2. The Open-Ended Question. The open-ended question is more general in nature. It tends to allow the respondent the flexibility to think, evaluate, and communicate where his or her own thought process and values lead. It usually elicits longer answers and helps to show your interest, when you listen quietly. It encourages the other person to express personal views, thoughts, interests, and feelings on the topic. Open-ended questions help the other person to look in-depth at some area which may not have been considered. These types of questions also provide the prober with a broad range and depth of information that can be used for immediate or later follow-up.

Examples: Tell me about... How...? In what way...? Can you explain...? Can you describe...? Why...? What is the reason for ...? Could you give me a picture of...? What thoughts do you have about...? What are your feelings about...?

Follow-up

Most people only scratch the surface when they probe. Most do not to follow up on their open-ended questions. A typical probing session conducted by an unsophisticated prober consists of the following:

1. Asking one open-ended question;
2. Getting a superficial, automatic response;
3. Asking a few directive questions;
4. Asking another **different** open-ended question;
5. Getting another automatic response, et cetera.

People who make the error of prematurely switching to a different open-ended question or prematurely firing away with directive questions have little idea how superficial the elicited information may be, or how much real and valuable information they might be passing up. Furthermore, the person being interviewed often feels he is either being interrogated or has not really been understood. Good probing does the following:

1. Establishes a solid base for good two-way communication;
2. Increases mutual respect and understanding;
3. Obtains a wealth of useful data about your client's needs—not only objective needs but also subjective needs, attitudes, and emotional state—information that may be an invaluable positioning tool and crucial to the negotiating process.

In many situations, negotiating or otherwise, the canned, automatic, fast responses to probing questions are knowingly or unknowingly superficial. Often, they misrepresent the real situation because they omit more than they disclose. Frequently, your client will be unaware of some aspect of his real needs. If the client had been fully aware of all the aspects of the situation, he probably would have satisfied his needs. Clarity about needs usually leads to rapid solutions and, subsequently, rapid sales.

Skillful in-depth probing cuts through the superficiality and determines what the person's real needs and aspirations are. Thus, the best follow-up to an open-ended question is a request for more communication on the same question. This approach guides the individual into looking with more depth at aspects they may not have previously thought about or noticed.

The result is that the person may achieve a realization of their real needs and some insights into how to handle them. They usually will feel good because, of course, it was their realization. They tend to regard you as competent and helpful. You now have a specific solution possibility that is very real to them. Of the, say, 12 benefits your service or product may offer, you now know the one or two that will most closely meet their perceived needs. Those are the ones you stress. You may be surprised about what ends up being significant. The other benefits may be mentioned, but they are far less important to that individual. Without probing for the individual's perception of need, you may neglect mentioning a benefit that is important to him or her. The important benefit to that individual was benefit number 11 out of 12 and, at least to you, it just did not seem important.

In-depth probing adds an important extra dimension and its value should not be under-estimated. Just because a person stops talking does not mean that there is not a lot more of importance to be said on a subject, or that you as the prober now know all there is to know.

To be a good prober, you must learn how to follow up. You must learn to **think in series.** All open-ended questions have series. When conducting in-depth probing, as the responses are given, you know what your next question will be. Simply ask for more on the same question. This is not a rote procedure. Keep to the original subject until you and the other person are satisfied that a complete and accurate picture has been presented. Be sure you have fully "heard" the person.

Examples of follow-up probes:
Example 1
"How...?" (Response)
"How else might... (Question 1)?" (Response)
"Are there any other ways... (Question 1)?" (Response)
Example 2
"What about...?" (Response)
"Anything else about... (Question 1)?" (Response)
"Are there any other thoughts/feelings/ideas
about... (Question 1)?" (Response)

Example 3

"Tell me about..." (Response)

"Tell me a more about... (Question l)" (Response)

"Can you go into that a little further?" (Response)

The main point here is that you do not stop with the first answer and move on to another question. After each response, you keep asking for a little more, other thoughts, feelings, and considerations. The person will start looking more closely and may come up with things of which even he or she wasn't aware. Remember, keep asking for more. It is easier and more comfortable than you think, once you get the hang of it. The information you obtain will amaze you. Keep doing it; keep asking for more until your counterpart definitively says that's the whole thing or all of a sudden smiles and says something to the effect of, "Gee, I just realized...," or "Gosh, I see now what the real situation is," exhibiting a new awareness of the issue. After all, it may never have been fully explored before! There is always more there than either party may consciously realize or even expect.

You may be surprised by the number of levels you can reach. Always keep in mind what the original question was and always get back to it. It even helps to write it down. Do not allow yourself to go off on tangents. Directive questions can be used to terminate a tangent or redirect attention. You may want to ask a few directive questions to get specific information as a point arises or simply to add variety to the communication.

Do not lapse into conversation—you can lose control of the process and forget your purpose and intention. You can ask an open-ended question about a more specific area as it comes up, and follow that to its conclusion. However, always return to the original question and follow it through. If the person continues to talk and show interest, don't interrupt, but do be sure to get your question answered. If the person is answering your question, it's best not to ask directive questions. You can always go back and get those specifics later. Wait for a pause. Do not interrupt unless you are obviously not getting your question answered. When you are getting an answer, listen.

Some Comments on Establishing Rapport

Like attracts like. When people are like each other they tend to like each other. Both the tone of your voice and your body language has a significant impact on how the other party receives your communication. In initially establishing rapport with someone, try to be aware of and try to match the voice tonality and body language of the other person. If the person is a fast talker and your pace tends to be slow, it would behoove you to speed it up. If the other person sits up straight and crosses his or her legs and you do the same, you create an image of being similar. You might be amazed at how these simple techniques combined with good listening skills will help set the foundation for making your probing easier and more fruitful. Like any technique, these can be abused. Always keep in mind that your intention when probing is to better understand and responsibly address all parties' needs.

Additional Comments on Getting More Information

In addition to being a good listener, there are some useful techniques for getting and keeping a person talking on a subject or for directing more talk on a subject area:

1. **Volunteer some information.** If you start the flow, the other person will usually respond in kind;

2. **Be silent.** Most people will continue to talk to fill the void. This, of course, should be handled with discretion;

3. **Provide partial acknowledgments.** This will show interest and indicate that you want the other person to continue. An occasional affirmative nod of the head, a soft "uh-huh" or "right" will keep the person talking. A full acknowledgment ("Good!

Thank you") says, in effect, "I fully understand what you said and you do not have to go on."

A premature acknowledgment (acknowledging someone before the have completed their communication) will also keep people talking, but only because they believe you could not possibly know all they had to say. It can make them feel frustrated and upset with you. Some people cut others off to save time or because they think they already know what the person is saying.

Upsets also occur when there is a lack of acknowledgment. This is often the cause of people talking until they are blue in the face. They do so because, since you did not acknowledge what they did say, they think you must not have understood. So they continue, hoping to hear an acknowledgement indicating that you understood;

4. **Repeat words or phrases.** Take a word or phrase from the last answer you got and repeat it in a questioning manner. For example, the person says, "I really enjoyed seeing the pink barn." You say, "Pink barn?" The individual will tend to expand on what you question by some statement like, "You know, the pink barn down by Sutter's Mill. It was up for sale last year, but Mr. Peterson got mad at his real estate agent and took it off the market. And do you know what? Last month they discovered oil on it...," etc.

Recap of Important Points

- Your primary intention should be to serve honestly the real needs and aspirations of the other party.
- Establish good rapport. Be present with interest and a willingness to listen.
- Don't assume you know, or that the other person's initial remarks have told you, what is actually needed.

- Probe **in-depth** to determine the other person's actual needs (from his or her point of view).
- As appropriate, align and emphasize benefits that meet specific perceived needs.
- If what you have to offer does not meet the other party's needs, refer him to something or someone who can help. Your helpfulness is often remembered.

The initial effort spent on in-depth probing will save you time in the long run. It not only will give you significantly more information about the other party's needs and underlying concerns, but also it will deepen the interpersonal connection. Why? Because in-depth probing demands excellent listening and acknowledgment skills, which act as validations of the other person and are always appreciated.

DEVELOPING A CONSULTATIVE RELATIONSHIP: A SALES EXAMPLE

Following is a brief example of how these communication concepts and principles are commonly violated. With willingness, intention, and practice, however, these violations can be easily redressed.

Most selling (especially when there is pressure for volume) consists of the following:

a. Knowing the products or services;
b. Establishing contact;
c. Making a presentation of the products or services;
d. Asking for an order.

Rote application of the above can degenerate into a hard-sell, used-car-salesman approach and image. A much better sequence of action that facilitates the development of a **consultative** relationship is as follows:

1. Know your products or services;
2. Establish contact and rapport. Be present and interested;
3. Observe, address, and acknowledge what the prospect has attention on **now;**
4. Determine the prospect's needs, from his or her point of view. Probe in-depth. Do not interrupt. Acknowledge appropriately;
5. Match the perceived needs of the prospect with the specific benefits of your services that are relevant to the prospect;
6. Close;
7. Ensure that what was promised is, delivered to the customer's satisfaction. Honor your commitments.

In most sales training and sales supervision the a–d sequence is usually emphasized. Any probing that is taught usually focuses on points that can position what the seller wants to sell without a comparable focus on determining what the buyer's perceived needs are from the buyer's viewpoint.

The suggested sequence (1–7) tends to be mishandled as follows: Although Point 1 is fundamental, its application varies greatly. Point 2 tends to be superficial and social. Point 3 is usually overlooked entirely. Point 4 often consists of asking a series of directive questions that the salesperson wants answered, which frequently have little relevance to the individual's perceived needs. Point 5 is usually not accomplished, because Point 4 was not adequately implemented. For example, the probing was not in-depth, there were too many interruptions, or there was a lack of appropriate acknowledgment. Because of the shortcomings mentioned above, Point 6, as compensation, tends to be manipulative and "technique-oriented" rather than natural. Point 7 is seldom consistently applied.

Observation tends to verify that when long-term positive relationships have developed, the salesperson has followed the above 1-7 sequence. This basic sequence, appropriately modified, is applicable to all forms of interpersonal interaction—from customer relations, sales, and negotiation to personal development and family relations.

SOME HELPFUL PROCESSES

The following processes can be amazingly effective but only if done with complete honesty and candor.

Communication Clearing Process

The purpose of the **communication clearing process** is to reduce misunderstandings and upsets and help move the communication toward greater dialogue. The person who is upset usually initiates this, but it can also be used simply to initiate a dialogue to gain more clarity on a topic. If one or both parties are upset, it's prudent to have this process facilitated by a neutral third party.

Willingness and **intention** on the part of both parties to be open to at least considering the viewpoints and perceptions of the other party are crucial to the effective use of this process. The viewpoints do not have to be accepted, but they must be considered or there is no dialogue, only rigid positions in opposition.

The sequence of dialogue, with only one personspeaking at a time and the other person listening, should progress as follows:

1. Be as present as possible;
2. Person A states the facts only;
2a. Person B states what he or she heard stated without evaluation or discussion. If needed, Person A clarifies for Person B anything missed or misunderstood. If appropriate, Person B is asked to repeat the clarification back to Person A;
3. Person A states his or her feelings (the emotional impact the facts had). Use "I" statements only—"I felt..." Do not use "You" statements—"You made me feel...", "You did...";
3a. Same as 2a;

4. Person A states any conclusions reached or judgments made;

4a. Same as 2a;

5. Person A states his or her request of what wanted, if anything, from Person B;

5a. Same as 2a;

6. Person A asks Person B if he or she would care to respond. If the answer is yes, Person A listens to and acknowledges what Person B says;

7. If appropriate, Person B may now share his or her interpretation of the event or situation per the same sequence.

It's amazing how much this simple process can do to dissipate upsets and conflicts in addition to adding clarity, allowance, understanding, appreciation, and mutual respect.

Self-Image Process

Most people don't take the time to figure out what their self-image is. This is critical to do. Our self-image defines the boundaries of what we are willing to experience. A rigid image based in some insecurity will severely limit our ability to capitalize on our much larger potential. If we are willing to stretch that image, then we can change and grow. This process can create profound change, but it must be done sincerely, without artifice. This process is personal and private. It is where we need to get very honest with ourselves.

1. Write paragraphs and paragraphs in a free flow of thought describing how you see yourself living your life. This is for your own private edification. You are not writing to impress anyone. Do not write only the good stuff or the bad stuff, but all the stuff. Be willing to look at and own it all. After all, it is the wholeness—the integrity—of your actual self-image for which you are trying to obtain clarity. You cannot change

what you will not confront. Wait 24 hours. Let it integrate.

2. Read what you wrote and condense it into one paragraph. Wait 24 hours.

3. Take the **concept** of what that paragraph expresses and condense it into one sentence or phrase. Wait 24 hours.

4. Condense that sentence or phrase to one word that expresses its essence. That is the old image. That is the image you have had of yourself, despite any pretenses or self-deception. It has been the boundary of what you have allowed yourself to be, to do, and to have. Wait 24 hours.

5. Reverse the process for your new image:

    a. Choose one word that expresses what you want your image to be. Wait 24 hours;

    b. Expand that word to one sentence. Wait 24 hours;

    c. Expand that sentence to one or two paragraphs. Wait 24 hours;

    d. Write paragraphs and pages with as much vivid detail as possible to describe how it would be living that image.

Once you have the details of that new image, **start living it emotionally**. Feel "as if" and act "as if." The fact will follow.

8
Facilitating Emotional Maturity

Maturity is a process not a destination. —Leo F. Buscaglia

GETTING INTO BALANCE

As in all things, when balance is missing we are unstable and insecure. We become defensive and our attention becomes narrow and self-centered. More of the greater world is excluded and our perceived universe becomes smaller and smaller. We experience a growing sense of difficulty dealing with the give-and-take of life, which makes us feel restricted and even less secure. We feel increasingly overwhelmed and out of control, which only leads to more imbalance and disharmony. Our perception of what we feel we need and want is correspondingly distorted. Therefore, **before** we can determine what we truly need and want, our consciousness needs to first move toward balance. Only then will we have the perspective of responsible action. **Without balance, all things are distorted, including what we think we need and want.**

Since we live in a dynamic universe, maturity is not about finding "the" balance, but rather is about a continual process of awareness and action toward balance and rebalances in the inevitable give-and-take of life.

But what is it we are balancing and rebalancing? We are harmonizing the energies of the areas our emotions are telling us need to be confronted to restore balance. When we ignore or repress our emotional messages, we stay out of balance and feel overwhelmed, which results in feeling bored, hostile, fearful, sad, despairing, or apathetic. How much time do you spend with these emotions? How balanced is your life?

The levels of emotional maturity give us a relative measurement of our balance. At Level 6 (see Chapter 6, *The Levels of Emotional Maturity*), we feel balanced and in harmony with and respond gracefully to the ebb and flow of life. As we move down the levels, we are less and less balanced, impacted with more discord, and feel mired in more areas of life.

Understanding our own emotional level helps us also discern from which emotional level another person is operating. This allows us to see more easily through social façades and more accurately determine that person's real attitudes and corresponding intentions. Because each emotional level has predictable associated attitudes and behaviors, once we understand a person's actual (not social) emotional state or level, we can also reliably predict behaviors not yet observed.

Remember, the lower the level, the greater the stress and sense of being overwhelmed and out of balance. Those feelings are indications that something needs to change. As we move down the levels, the need for change increases, as does a corresponding resistance to change. With experience, we can start to discern the more subtle differences within the levels themselves. This differentiation provides clarity as to where we need to focus our attention to begin moving toward more balance in our lives. This enhances our ability to make more effective choices including the kind of communication or intervention that would be most effective in interacting with a particular individual.

As a reminder, the underlying emotions themselves, their order, and their relationships to each other are the same for all human beings, regardless of personality, gender or cultural differences. As important as these differences are, they all function within the universal emotional framework.

EMOTIONAL STATES
Acute Emotional States

An acute emotional state is the actual present-time emotion associated with a specific experience, that is, how we are feeling right **now**. We all have our acute ups and downs, day to day, moment to moment, that indicate to us (if we listen) how we are perceiving and responding or reacting to our environment in that moment. All of us, at different times, have experienced the entire hierarchy of emotions, from apathy and despair, to fear and anger, to contentment, enthusiasm, and joy.

Chronic Emotional States

Our chronic emotional state is our emotional "home base"—the one we return to when the acute emotional ups and downs settle out. Recurring attitudes and behaviors, beyond a person's social façade, such as "always angry," or "happy and positive most of the time," or "usually sad," reflect and are manifestations of a person's chronic state. Where our home base resides on the levels of emotional maturity is a very strong indication of our level of responsibility and, therefore, our resiliency and effectiveness in dealing with the circumstances of life.

Once we understand the emotional hierarchy, and as we become familiar with an individual's home base, when we observe acute departures from it, up or down, we can reliably predict the emotions and behavior the person will go through as the he or she returns to home base. The intensity with which and how fast or slow individuals move will vary, but the emotions and behaviors they go through will not. The higher the home base, the more responsive (versus reactive), resilient, and happier an individual is.

A individual's willingness to feel the entire range of emotions, by itself, raises that person's **emotional home base.** The higher an individual's emotional home base, the greater the person's real presence and, thus, responsiveness to and resiliency in constructively dealing with any situation. Facilitating movement that raises the emotional home base effectively raises the level of emotional maturity. This is true for both individuals and organizations.

Social Demeanor

Both acute and chronic emotional states can be significantly different from the social demeanor we assume for public view. That social demeanor may be higher, lower, or the same as our actual acute or chronic emotional state.

Social competence and behavior depends largely on social background and personality. Different personalities exhibit different social interaction skills, but all can be more or less emotionally intelligent. Though social competence may have socially desirable aspects and benefits, it does not necessarily correlate to a person's level of emotional maturity. What does correlate is the degree to which the person engages in authentic communication and responsible behavior.

In a society that tends to cover up actual emotions, we often present a social demeanor or façade that broadcasts a message different from how we are actually feeling. The ability to differentiate an individual's acute emotional state from a social demeanor, when they differ, is an aspect of being emotionally intelligent and is crucial to effective interaction in any arena, personal or professional.

Cultural Influences

Cultural, political, and social demands have an impact on what we think and how readily we allow ourselves to feel. Unfortunately, much of society not only condones but often encourages repression of feeling.

Graciousness and consideration for other people's feelings are wonderful qualities. However, far too often, being polite or socially correct is not gracious or sensitive at all, but rather is a rationalization used to avoid honest expression of feelings.

Each culture, in various ways, limits some aspects of authentic emotional expression. This may have some seemingly socially desirable effects, but it always results in limitations that are, ultimately, detrimental to the individual and to society.

EMOTIONAL RANGE AND FACILITATION LEVEL

"Facilitation level" is the emotional communication that recipients can both relate to and be motivated by, given their acute emotional state. In any particular emotional state, people have a limited range of what makes sense to them. That range of emotional reality is typically no greater than one level away from a person's acute (not social) emotional state. People will be more or less receptive or motivated, depending on how much a communication falls within their emotional range. Effective facilitation requires being willing and able to adapt our communication so as to relate somewhat above the other person's acute emotional state but within his or her emotional range.

Attempting to relate to, influence, motivate, lead, or persuade by communicating outside a person's acute emotional range simply will not work. In other words, relating to people via their social demeanor, when that is significantly different from their acute emotional state, will not be effective. Not only will it be ineffective, but it will actually inhibit further communication, because the person will be turned off by how unreal the message is. The recipient will, in fact, be more negative to the presenter, to the viewpoint of the presenter, and to whomever or whatever the presenter is representing. This is valid for written as well as oral communication.

Developing skills at applying the appropriate facilitation level is integral to enhancing motivational and leadership abilities.

UNDERSTANDING FACILITATION DYNAMICS

Following is a partial review of emotions and communication:

1. Emotions are messages from our subconscious about how well we're surviving. They are not good or bad, but they do indicate relative degrees of security or stress;

2. Each emotion has a different filter of perception associated with predictable beliefs, perceived needs, attitudes, intentions, and behaviors;

3. Individuals perceive and respond or react to life circumstances from their acute (not social) emotional state;

4. Individuals have a limited range of perception around their acute emotion;

5. Communication outside an individual's emotional range of perception will not be real, motivating, or effective for that person. It will tend to be the opposite;

6. Communication at an emotional level just above an individual's acute emotional state or level and within the individual's emotional range of reality will be real, motivating, and effective for that person;

7. Personal growth, that is, becoming more emotionally mature and acting with integrity more of the time, is about moving one's "home base" to a higher level.

Lack of awareness of these points or unwillingness to apply them can lead to a canned, inflexible style of communication or presentation. No matter how smooth or sophisticated the presentation may be, it will be effective only to the extent it falls within the emotional range and, thus, reality of the recipient.

To reiterate and emphasize this critical point: if our communication falls outside the emotional range and reality of the person with whom we are communicating, it will not be effective in leading, motivating, or persuading that person. Furthermore, it will more likely result in the opposite. If we end up getting what we want by communicating outside a person's (or a group's) acute emotional range, we were successful for other reasons and in spite of, rather than because of, our communication.

To the degree that we can competently assess a person's real level of emotional maturity, we have a powerful means to determine accurately the likelihood of certain behaviors. We then can determine how to most effectively communicate and deal with that person.

Table 6.2, Chapter 6, page 158, The Levels of Emotional Maturity, describes attitudinal and behavioral characteristics associated with each of the six levels of emotional maturity. The level where most of the observed current behavior occurs is a good initial indication of a person's probable acute emotional level. Observations over time will determine the person's chronic level or home base. Once the person's chronic level is established, we can predict with a high degree of accuracy and reliability other attitudes and behaviors not yet observed but highly likely to be present at that level.

Our acute behavior can range through all six levels, sometimes quite quickly. Acutely, we can be cheerful one moment, sad the next and angry shortly thereafter. However, chronic behavior will seldom stray more than one level from home base.

When there appears to be more than one level difference manifested in a number of different behaviors, it is usually an indication that the higher level is an attempted social cover-up of the actual lower level. For example, observations of a number of behaviors over time, some of which appear to be at Level 5 or 6 and others which are indicative of Level 2 behaviors, strongly indicate an attempt to disguise negative intentions and behavior. High-level individuals are human and have their ups and downs; however, they do not **chronically** manifest low-level behavior in any arena.

COMMUNICATING WITH REALITY

The types of communication and the behaviors that will be most real to the person (or group) with whom we are communicating are those associated with the level on which that person (or group) is operating at the time. If we match the other person's emotional state when communicating, there will tend to be strong rapport: "People like people who are like themselves." Conversely, the further our communication strays from the other person's emotional state, the less rapport we will have, and the less effective we are likely to be.

If we communicate at a slightly higher emotional level but within the other person's emotional range, the rapport will be slightly less, but respect and motivating influence will be greater. People are easily influenced by the next higher level. However, attempts to communicate at more than one level removed from where the person is will likely result in alienation and misunderstanding. Remember that the lower the emotional level, the greater the stress and insecurity and the less the certainty and confidence an individual is experiencing, regardless of pretenses to the contrary.

True dialogue does not occur at the lower levels, for at those levels individuals are insecure and, as a result, often deceive and manipulate. True dialogue, with its openness and honesty, only occurs at Levels 5 and 6, where individuals are secure, open to, and truly interested in listening to and learning from other viewpoints.

Observing where a person is within the emotional levels and facilitating his movement up them, without skipping any level, helps that person reach a more productive and happier emotional state. A person does not jump from apathy or fear, for example, to strong interest or enthusiasm. An individual's emotional state changes by going through each successive emotional level in sequential order.

APPLYING THE APPROPRIATE FACILITATION LEVEL

Consider this example of how to apply an appropriate facilitation level. If a person is displaying generalized opposition with an angry tone, that individual is likely behaving at the lower end of Level 3. Our immediate goal is to get the generalized hostility more focused. Understanding that the Opposer's behavior is a defense against some perceived threat, we need, without accusation or attack, to help the person become more focused on the specifics of his anger. For example, ask, "What specifically happened?" "How many times—exactly?" "Who specifically?" Asking non-threatening questions that narrow the focus of the person's anger to specifics provides him or her with an opportunity to ventilate hostility without being made wrong. Becoming more focused and specific also provides the person (and you) with something concrete to evaluate and do something about.

Continuing to ask for more, in a non-threatening manner, helps to move a person into neutral, as he feels his or her concerns have been heard and acknowledged. Moving on by mentioning some facts that may be of interest to the person helps to move him to a state of curiosity. Providing relevant data interests the person even more. Continuing in this vein may even bring the person to a feeling of enthusiasm.

As another example, if we detect hints of covert behavior or subtle untruths (Level 2), an effective facilitating response is to display a willingness to use overt hostile force (Level 3) against the perceived problem. Why? Because the individual is feeling hostility but is too afraid to express it. He relates to the hostility and admires someone else who is willing to overtly express what he or she is too afraid to express. The person communicating at the slightly higher level serves as a model, and effectively as a leader, thereby encouraging more direct expression and action by the other party.

Note that we have attempted to raise the other person's acute emotional state gradually, by doing the following:

- Understanding the behavioral characteristics of each emotion and the relationships among the levels of emotional maturity;

- Being aware of the person's actual (not social) present-time emotional state;

- Communicating (without judgment or "attitude") from the emotions and attitudes of the level just above the other person's acute emotional state. Communication from that slightly higher level tends to bring the person up to that level;

- Once the person has come up to a higher level, the facilitator then shifts and communicates from the next higher level, repeating the process until the person is communicating at least at Level 4, preferably Level 5 or Level 6.

The same process is used at the lowest level. A person who is apathetic is below grief. Helping to focus that person's attention on the loss, which will be the focus of the person's grief, is actually positive and therapeutic. Why? Because in a state of apathy or despair, the person has a "why bother, don't care, nothing we can do anyway" attitude. If we can get the person to recall a time of loss, that person will have greater emotional involvement than before, which is therapeutic. Similarly, helping a person move from grief to feeling sorry for him- or herself is a process of expanding both the person's feelings and awareness. This process is very helpful to the person, even if initially counterintuitive.

Continuing in this manner increasingly expands awareness. At Level 1, people are almost totally self-centered and emotionally introverted. Moving them into fear is the next step, as it directs their attention beyond themselves. By doing this, we help to make them aware of the dangers of staying where they were, and we help thaw their numbness. Only with this awareness can they hope to do something about the danger (at first covertly, as they are initially too afraid to be overt). As they become stronger, they become more willing to be open and direct with their hostility. At each progressive stage, individuals feel more able to have an impact. The lower emotional levels may not be pretty, but "the way out is the way through." Understanding the emotional hierarchy and its associated behaviors provides clarity as to which way is "out."

We can raise the question, "Isn't using facilitation levels being manipulative, which would relegate us to Level 2 ourselves?" That statement assumes manipulation is purely bad. In evaluating good or bad, it's important to look to the underlying intention. Is the intention positive, caring, or helpful, or is it negative, hostile, or hurtful? Outward behavior can be misleading or deceiving. Before judging behavior, if possible, always look to the intention. At minimum, looking for the underlying intention tends to expand perspective. But, remember, if the evaluator's acute emotion is in the lower levels, their evaluation will be biased toward the negative. Only at Levels 5 and 6 will the evaluation be relatively objective and free of bias. This is simply another reason why doing what we can to raise the level of emotional maturity is so important.

CHRONIC LOW-LEVEL BEHAVIOR

Use of facilitation level can elegantly expedite chronically high-level people who are momentarily overwhelmed to more quickly regain their perspective and power. The higher the chronic level, the greater the resilience of the individual when acutely stressed and, therefore, the easier and more effective the use of facilitation level.

If moving a person to the higher levels at the present time is not possible, then moving the person out of the current environment (including termination) should be considered. Why? Because, while in the lower levels, people's behavior is more destructive than constructive, both to themselves and their surroundings. Because the person is reactive rather than responsive, present-time decisions and actions will be negatively skewed. If the person is at work, it is often better to send the person home and pay him or her rather than allow the person to continue to do more damage, which is being done even though it may not be immediately apparent. In addition, a change in environment can lessen the re-stimulation of whatever is causing the reactivity, more easily allowing facilitation. This change is often helpful, unless the stimulation originated in the environment to which the person is being sent.

Although the skillful use of facilitation level can be markedly beneficial in an acute situation, using facilitation level to move individuals who are chronically stuck in the lower three levels is problematic and will have, at best, limited short-term effect. Remember, as dysfunctional as that may be, people chronically stuck in a lower level have found, within that level, a way to survive. Consequently, they tend to be extremely reluctant to give it up. Such people need more than good motivating communication. We can provide a safe environment. We can encourage. We can communicate our concerns. We can initiate various interventions. Nevertheless, when push gets to shove, no one changes until that person, individually makes that choice. Until he or she does so, all outside attempts will fail no matter how competent or well intended they are.

The best thing you can do for yourself and your organization is not to allow a chronic low-level individual to continue operating in your space. Do what is necessary to remove such individuals from the environment. This does not mean giving them a good evaluation or reference just to more easily get rid of them. That's irresponsible. Remove them, responsibly. Do it with sensitivity, do it legally—but do it. Unwillingness to confront individuals chronically functioning on the lower levels is one of the most common and costly avoidances. Organizationally, it indicates marginally effective management at best.

If we are to be responsible, effective leaders, managers, or just plain good friends, it is imperative that we not allow or contribute directly or indirectly to the continuation of low-level behavior. To do so is hurtful to all parties. Realize that being a "good guy," being "reasonable" or "polite" about ignoring, tolerating, or allowing chronic low-level behavior is not doing anyone any kindness—it is just the opposite. It is cowardly and is irresponsible.

Leaders who tolerate or ignore lower-level behaviors do so either out of ignorance or out of lower-level behavior themselves. If the reason is ignorance, then they need to be educated as to the destructive consequences of their "reasonable, nice-guy" behavior. Chronic lower-level manifestation in anyone needs to be corrected expeditiously or the individual's employment terminated. Allowing lower-level behavior to persist is always destructive to all parties.

THE LEVELS AND INTERVENTION EFFECTIVENESS

An understanding of the characteristics of emotional levels provides us with an increased ability to determine, for each individual, the potential effectiveness of various interventions. The higher the level of emotional maturity, the greater an individual's sense of security, self-esteem, and self-confidence. Correspondingly, the greater is an individual's ability to integrate and utilize new data and skills. Below Level 4 individuals are in overwhelm and unable to integrate new information.

Thus, most interventions conducted in the lower levels are an inefficient use of resources. The exception is competently conducted therapy (for those willing). Significant gains tend to occur primarily above Level 3. As the individual becomes healthier, therapy may no longer be needed and competent coaching, mentoring, training, or consulting takes on increasingly effective roles (see Figure 8.1 next page).

FIGURE 8.1
The Effectiveness of Competently Conducted Interventions
with Individuals at Various Levels of Emotional Maturity

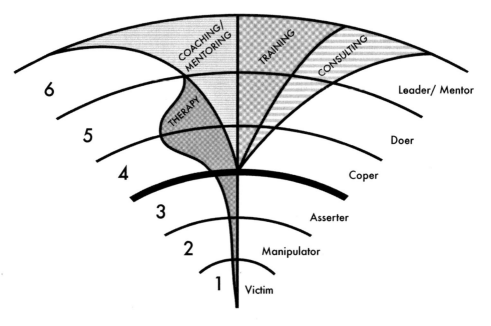

UNDERSTANDING PERSONALITY, GENDER AND CULTURAL DIFFERENCES

The Levels of Emotional Maturity are the same for all people regardless of differences in personality, gender or cultural background. All people move up or down via the same emotional levels. However, differences in personality, gender and culture do affect how each person does so. Sensitivity to these different arenas increase rapport. It also adds valuable, and sometime necessary, precision in dealing with people at different levels of emotional maturity. The more one understands these factors and their variations, the less likely misunderstandings will occur and the greater the potential for effective and meaningful interaction.

Personality theories and models abound. A particularly useful model is the Enneagram of Personality. An ancient model of the mystery schools, it was available for centuries only to the elite few. Since the mid 1980s, dozens of books on it have become available. Educators, trainers and presenters may find particular interest in the *Enneagram Intelligences* by Janet Levine, which focuses on the different learning needs of the various personalities. A book specifically integrating the nine different personality types or drives with the six levels of emotional maturity is currently in process by yours truly and will be available in 2006.

Men and women do have different perspectives on a number of issues. Obviously, it is helpful, sometimes critical, to understand those differences. You may want to start with John Gray's popular *Men are from Mars, Women are from Venus*.

Understanding and dealing with cultural differences is too broad an arena, within the confines of this book, to make specific recommendations but is a vitally important aspect too often innocently or arrogantly overlooked.

THE VALUE OF COMPETENT COACHING

The impact of providing training and consulting services to and receiving them from emotionally mature individuals is great. Having the right kind of coaching is essential. Coaching to evoke and instill a skill set works well in certain areas, such as emergency preparedness and sports. However, coaching with the goal of helping others to determine what they really want, access their inherent talents, empower themselves, bring their lives into greater balance, and thus be happier more of the time is more complex. It is a different process and requires different competencies.

Developing competence in this latter kind of coaching is one of the most effective and efficient ways an organization can improve both performance and morale. Coaching competence is an invaluable tool for any supervisor, manager, or executive. It should be a key element of any comprehensive management or leadership development program. It is especially valuable for people who mentor others.

Without coaching competence, mentoring tends to deteriorate into little more than political sponsorship.

Coaching has many aspects, but most of all it is about assisting individuals in recognizing and using more of their inherent strengths and talents. It is about facilitating people's growth and helping them manifest their potential. It is not about instructing people on how to do something or doing it for them. It is about facilitating other people's willingness to be more responsible, accountable, and empowered. Coaching is about helping individuals help themselves and, in the process, enjoy life more.

Often, when individuals seek coaching, it is to acquire assistance in addressing some area of perceived limitation. The challenge of coaching is to refrain from letting the process focus on problem solving or conflict resolution. Certainly, problems need to be addressed and solved or resolved. However, that is not the purpose of coaching or the role of a coach.

The purpose of coaching is not to solve problems but to help individuals better understand themselves—how and why they do what they do. It is to help them figure out how they create personal limitations, and how to take increasingly more responsibility for their own condition, and change it if they so choose. Coaching is about helping individuals focus on recognizing, understanding, and taking ownership of the causal factors that influence their behavior.

Frequently, the presenting issue is only a symptom of something more fundamental that the client has not yet observed or confronted. Fixing the symptom may provide temporary relief but seldom resolves the underlying issue. Competent coaching includes having the skills and flexibility to look beyond the obvious and use the presenting issue in such a way that the client learns and grows in the process. In fact, everything that comes up is part of the process and can be used to help the individual become more aware and responsible and, thus, more powerful. Coaching is like peeling an onion, uncovering the layers of a social persona, going beneath the "shoulds and oughts," bringing to light the repressed or unspoken fears. It is helping the individual create a willingness to faces their fears. With that develops the ability to move through and beyond the fears, to discover and release more of their dormant capabilities.

Competent coaching recognizes individual differences in needs, communication abilities, emotional maturity, and personality. Understanding the human dynamics involved and how to deal with those differences is the key to effectively relating to, educating as needed and motivating each unique individual.

The steps outlined below are suggested primarily to ensure that all the important basics to effective coaching are covered. Each step lays a foundation for the next. Once we have laid the overall foundation, various steps may be returned to and reinforced. However, a coach's primary attention should be on the needs of the client, not on any blind adherence to a process. Being present and attuned to the client's needs and responsibly adapting to them is a coach's senior priority.

1. Create a safe space where candor and confidentiality is the honored norm.
2. Help the client sort through the "shoulds and oughts" to find and clarify what he truly needs and wants.
3. Mutually determine the parameters of the coaching relationship.
4. Assist the individual to more clearly recognize and own the impact of her behavior.
5. Determine the broader contribution(s) that that person can and wants to make. Assess and prioritize.
6. Facilitate expanded commitment to responsible proactive behavior.
7. Encourage greater responsibility and accountability for one's own needs, actions and commitments. Acknowledge and celebrate doing so.

As the coaching process progresses, personal consideration of what is "wanted" often evolves from initial attention on functional skills improvement to a deeper focus on determining, developing, and aligning core values and purpose. Improved interpersonal relations and increased personal satisfaction frequently are byproducts of the process.

On occasion, this coaching process reveals that the needs of the individual and the organization are not in alignment. Unless they move into alignment, it is usually better for the individual to leave the organization so that he or she can get on with doing what is more fulfilling. It is better for the organization in that the job is now open to an individual potentially more aligned with the organization's needs. When individual and organizational goals and values are not in alignment, mediocre performance is the predictable result. All parties are frustrated and unhappy. Consequently, a non-aligned individual is more of a liability than an asset.

A coach is a facilitator, an ally, a cheerleader, a devil's advocate and a trusted friend. His or her main purpose is to help the individual determine and attain more of what she truly wants and, as appropriate, to help her align those desires and aspirations with the needs and goals of the organization. If those align, the result is a much happier, enthusiastic, and empowered producer. That individual is much more likely to contribute in ways that optimize benefits to **both** the individual and the organization.

In summary, a coach's job is to help individuals become more of who they really are by assisting them to:

- Clarify their values, needs, and aspirations;
- Recognize, take responsibility for, and change limiting patterns of behavior;
- Recognize, acknowledge, and more fully develop their inherent strengths and talents;

- Empower themselves to greater, more responsible actions;
- Determine how they can (or cannot) better align with and contribute to an organization's needs and goals;
- Challenge themselves to grow and hold themselves accountable for their own needs, actions, and commitments.

There are a number of well-regarded coach training organizations; check the internet for websites. My personal experience with The Coaches Training Institute (www.TheCoaches.com) was very positive. Also, see The International Coach Federation (www.coachfederation.org). Suggested readings: *Co-Active Coaching* by Whitworth, Kimsey-House and Sandahl; *Masterful Coaching* by Robert Hargrow; *The Art and Practice of Leadership Coaching* by Howard May; *Effective Coaching: Lessons from the Coach's Coach* by Myles Downey.

The greatest good you can do for another is not just to share your riches, but to reveal to him his own. —Benjamin Disraeli

"STUCK" LEADERSHIP

Individual leadership styles, attitudes, and motivations vary greatly. However, effective motivators have one thing in common: they all have learned to relate at an emotional level that meets the emotional needs of their audience for something better.

The result of that leadership can be positive or negative. The crucial underlying factor that determines whether a leader's impact will be positive is his or her chronic emotional level, which defines and describes the limits of that person's world view and range of corresponding attitudes. If the leader's chronic emotional level is high, the attitudes and outcome will be positive and constructive. If the leader's chronic emotional level is low, those aspects predictably will be negative and destructive.

Leadership is a dynamic process of keeping others reaching and moving beyond where they are. Part of that process involves the leader accurately assessing the constituents' emotional level, communicating slightly above that level, drawing the audience up. The leader offers or models what the audience perceives as something better. He continues that process, gradually moving his audience up the levels of emotional maturity to higher states of awareness, responsibility, and accountability. When that process stops, leadership, per se, stops.

If a leader is able to motivate a person or a group that is acutely in the lower emotional levels, the leader must continue the process as long as it takes, until the followers are at a responsible emotional level (Level 4 and above). If the leader stops at any of the lower levels, he or she tends to plant the followers in those negative levels, only now the followers are more energized. The consequences of that energy will be irresponsible and destructive. A classic example of this is Hitler, who though probably psychotic himself, adroitly used angry rhetoric and policies to motivate an overwhelmed population from grief and fear into the aggression of Level 3—and stuck them there. Motivating people has consequences and responsibilities. "The way out is the way through"— all the way through to the higher levels where responsible behavior resides.

If you start to take Vienna—take Vienna. —Napoleon Bonaparte

Chronic low-level behavior is fundamentally insecure, and therefore self-centered, hostile, lacking in compassion, and abusive. Individuals, groups, organizations, or nations stuck in the lower levels do destructive things. They ultimately self-destruct, but in the process, the collateral damage can be huge.

THE POWER AND SCOPE OF FACILITATION DYNAMICS

The power and potential effectiveness of the appropriate use of facilitation level is by no means restricted to individuals or small groups. The dynamics and applicability of facilitation level are universal and cross-cultural, macrocosmically as well as microcosmically. They apply to motivating huge populations as well as to individuals.

Facilitating principles and dynamics themselves are neutral. That is, when competently applied, they are effective whether the person using them is ethical, unethical, sane, or insane. They simply work and are applicable in virtually any context. Thus, like most powerful tools, they can be used or abused. Human ignorance or abuse of them can be and has been devastating, as Hitler (and history) has demonstrated. Being aware of facilitation dynamics assists us in understanding what is actually taking place. We then have a much better chance of using those dynamics constructively. Our ability in assessing the dysfunctional leaders and destructive despots of the world as well as irresponsible people in our environment expands. They can no longer easily seduce us by their rhetoric. Competent and responsible use of the appropriate facilitation level—summarized in table 8.1, page 212—to expedite a person's movement toward increased emotionally mature behavior is a win for everybody.

THE DNA OF CONTRIBUTION

TABLE 8.1: FACILITATION DYNAMICS

LEVEL	Range of Emotional Behavior	Attitude/ Behavior	To Move from:
6	From cheerful to enthusiastic (very strong, focused interest).	Act with integrity above all else.	Level 6 to integration
5	From mild to strong interest.	Be conscientious and responsible.	Level 5 to Level 6
4	From neutral to contentment.	Do the minimum to get by.	Level 4 to Level 5
3	From generalized overt hostility to specific overt hostility.	Attack the "enemy"; "get them before they get us."	Level 3 to Level 4
2	From fear to unexpressed resentment.	Manipulate the "enemy"; "con them before they con us."	Level 2 to Level 3
1	From "nothing anyone can do about it," through despair and grief, to feeling sorry for oneself.	Appease the "enemy" or do nothing.	Level 1 to Level 2

Focus of Facilitator	Reason for Doing So
Encourage an in-depth look at what truly "turns them on"—help them find their own passion/ambition versus those of parents or society.	Much of people's "dissatisfaction," regardless of material/social success, is in "living" other people's dreams/ ambitions rather than their own or being "practical" rather than doing what they're passionate about.
Expand arena and degree of proactive, responsible interests and behaviors; encourage greater dialogue.	Joy, happiness and aliveness are about being willing to face and experience more of life's richness and depth.
Encourage action from passive neutrality to increased proactive interests and behaviors.	Neutrality and contentment are static states; they inevitably will deteriorate into frustration unless interests are proactively developed.
Encourage and request specificity in recognizing and communicating what the upset is about.	Increasing focus on specifics provides substance to deal with and the communication about them ventilates hostility and helps move the person toward neutrality.
Be direct; call them on their manipulative behaviors, e.g., "Stop the pretenses, I know what you're doing!" Encourage them to become more candid with their hostility.	Based in fear, they are afraid to be overt in their hostility but admire the "bravery" of someone who is willing to express the hostility they feel. Calling them on their covert manipulations often gets them overtly angry—a healthy movement.
Acknowledge the apathy, despair, grief, or self-pity present; bring them up to the fear that inaction will have even bigger consequences; encourage them to express the accompanying hostility.	Emotions at this level tend to be paralyzing; eliciting a fearful expression of hostility against the real or imagined oppressor starts movement.

Table 8.2- The Levels Of Emotional Maturity—Organzational Aspects

		AA Handling Of Politics Within Organizations	AB Reliability
Level 6 Leader	True Power	Politics on this level means understanding that individuals and groups have unique needs. Also, that one needs to be aware of these differences and must have sensitivity and the appropriate communication skills necessary to get positive, ethical results for all concerned. Uses "politics" in the most positive sense of the word.	Honors commitments. Delivers as promised or if no longer possible, makes appropriate restitution.
Level 5 Doer		Less of above. Somewhat more "reasonable" in rationalizing and justifying behavior to accommodate personal positioning.	Usually dependable and reliable.
Level 4 Coper	False "Power" / "Power Over" / Powerless	The "ho-hum," "go with the flow," non-involved observer. The "non-politician." Can't be "bothered" with playing politics at any level. Feeling they are "above" politics when they are actually simply non-responsive and non-committed about most things.	Marginal.
Level 3 Opposer		Blames own inadequacies on "those rotten politicians." Hostility and overt opposition often rationalized as, "I'm just frank and honest." Belligerence will "turn off" those at higher levels but a dynamic speaker at this level can easily appear charismatic and persuasive to an audience in fear. (example: Hitler)	Unreliable.
Level 2 Manipu- lator		"Politician" in the worst sense of the word. Can attain great heights in organizations through "charm," manipulation, lies, claiming undeserved credit, and shifting responsibility for own shortcomings to others. Although always a major liability to the organization despite appearances, the total real costs are seldom apparent. No real loyalties except to self.	Will NOT deliver as promised. Artful cover-ups and excuses. Devious.
Level 1 Victim		Too weak and too much of a crybaby or "yes man" to be really political. Rather, propitiates to the manipulator or apparent power "hoping" to get by. Sense that there is nothing one can do except "go along."	Cannot be depended upon in any way.

AC Handling of Problems/ Degree of Overwhelm	AD Leadership and Management Potential and Contribution	AE Responsible Management Action (if behavior chronic)		
Views "problems" as challenges and opportunities to learn and grow. Emphasis on solution vs. problem. Resolutions often elegant and creative.	Outstanding. "The emotionally wise leader." Should be given every organizational opportunity/ advantage possible.	Acknowledge. Reward. Support. Promote.	Leadership	**Level 6 Leader**
Deals with most situations effectively.	Good to very good especially with Level 6 coaching and mentoring.	Acknowledge/confront as appropriate. Support/Mentor. Coach/Train. Reward.		**Level 5 Doer**
Problems are a bother. Ignores them if possible. Copes with them if can't avoid them. "It's someone else's job." "Camouflaged hole."	Poor to Fair. Generally not managerial material, but potentially could progress with excellent leadership & coaching.	Confront. Coach/Train. If they move to Level 5, acknowledge, reward and support; if not, terminate.	↓	**Level 4 Coper**
Feeling overwhelmed. Fights/rejects viable solutions. Refuses to take responsibility for their contribution to the problems—instead blames others.	Destructive."Leads," "man-ages," by threat and intimida-tion. Weak leadership often ignores, allows or condones such behavior, rationalizing "their numbers are up"—a short term "fix" that doesn't confront the real costs of such destruc-tive behavior.	**Terminate.** Be careful to distinguish between the behavior of a chronic level 3 person and that of level 5 or 6 person whose style/personality may be direct and overtly, but responsibly, demanding. The apparent similarities are superficial. The concerns and values are significantly different.	Lack Of / Destructive "Leadership"	**Level 3 Opposer**
Heavy overwhelm, despera-tion often skillfully covered. Pretends to deal with problems, but doesn't. Covertly misdirects responsi-bility to others. Manipulates self into position to take credit for other's solutions.	Very Destructive. Threatened by and undermines those that are highly competent. Pro-motes/rewards incompetence. Should not be allowed to lead or manage under any circum-stances.	**Terminate.** Retaining known chronic manipulators is an exercise in fearful avoidance, self-sabotaging rationalization, managerial irresponsibility and organizational destruc-tion.		**Level 2 Manipu-lator**
Totally overwhelmed. "Nothing I can do about it."	Zero.	**Terminate.**	↓	**Level 1 Victim**

OVERVIEW OF FACILITATION LEVEL

We can help an individual (or group) raise his emotional state by recognizing the individual's acute emotional level and consciously choosing to relate in ways that communicate aspects of the next higher level (facilitating level). Skipping levels usually is ineffective, as too high a jump seems unreal and out of reach to the other person.

Skillful use of the appropriate facilitation level can be amazingly effective in any supervisory, motivational, or leadership role, be it one-to-one or en masse. If we observe otherwise healthy individuals drop into the lower levels, competent application of the facilitation level may be the most helpful thing we can do for both the individual and the organization. The individual benefits, because she is miserable in the lower levels, despite any denials, pretenses, rationalizations, or arguments to the contrary. The organization benefits because the individual in the lower level is being destructive not only to herself but also to her environment.

Although the levels of emotional maturity are universal and cross-cultural, each individual has a unique variation on the underlying emotional dynamic. The human dynamic is complex and, as such, quick fixes and rote procedures seldom work. Developing skill in facilitating someone up the levels is not a rote procedure. It requires an ability to recognize, through social performances and pretenses, the person's actual emotional state. To the extent that we understand the attitudes and behaviors, including likely resistances, which correspond to each emotional state, we can more accurately understand that individual's perception of reality, including the individual's motivations and perceived needs. Even with understanding the characteristics of and relationships among the emotional levels, developing facilitation expertise takes practice and persistence. **However, for those willing to invest the effort, the rewards can be profound.**

Epilogue
A Call to Leadership

Creating an integral environment is
the ultimate leadership success.

Recent advances in understanding the human dynamic provide more tools and opportunities than ever before to influence the world positively. With the resources at their disposal, enlightened leaders can generate a paradigm shift of enormous significance. How? By doing their best to access these tools and use them to facilitate emotional maturity and integrity within their existing sphere of influence, whatever that may be.

Our integrity is the essence of who we are. Our well-being and sense of fulfillment are the result of how much we are in touch with that essence. The levels of emotional maturity provide an indication of just how much we are or are not.

Understanding the levels enhances our ability to facilitate our personal growth and that of others – if they and we so choose. It does always get down to our individual and personal choice. No one can facilitate anyone unless that person chooses to be facilitated. Anything else is coercive manipulation. Facilitate the maturity of willing individuals and you help develop people who make choices that are more responsible. Do so and you create a saner, more secure, mature, productive and happier environment.

If even a few people in your immediate surroundings were a little more secure, a little more responsible, what would happen?

Imagine the possibilities. Doesn't it behoove us to do whatever we can to facilitate ourselves, our loved ones, and our associates in that direction? Shouldn't we be doing our best to create an environment that attracts, develops, supports, and requires emotionally mature people of integrity? Doing so is a process that requires awareness and skills. The intention of this book is to encourage and assist in that process.

Admittedly, the challenge is significant—daunting for many. Why? Because, any real change initially creates confusion, doubt, and fear. Predictably, there will be resistance and pressure to hang on to old, familiar patterns. But, **for those up to the challenge of playing a more purposeful game, creating an integral environment is the ultimate leadership success. The means are available.** What is needed is leadership intention and commitment. **Are you up to the challenge?**

For all the sad words of tongue or pen the saddest are these: It might have been. —John Greenleaf Whittier

Suggested Reading

Almaas, A., *The Pearl Beyond Price,* Diamond Books, 1988.

Bennis, W., *On Becoming a Leader,* Addison-Wesley, 1989.

Bossidy, L. and Charan, R., *Execution,* Crown Business, 2002.

Capra, F., *The Turning Point,* Simon & Schuster, 1988.

Hartman, T., *Attention Deficit Disorder: A Different Perception.*
  Underwood Books, 1993.

Charan, R. and Tichy, N., *Every Business Is a Growth Business,*
  Random House, 1998.

Collins, J. and Porras, J., *Built to Last,* HarperCollins, 1994.

Davis, R. and Braun, E., *The Gift of Dyslexia,*
  Berkeley Publishing Group, 1994.

DePree, M., *Leadership Is an Art,* Doubleday, 1990.

Dyer, W., *The Power of Intention: Learning to Co-Create
  Your World Your Way,* Hay House, 2004.

George, B., *Authentic Leadership: Rediscovering the Secrets to
  Creating Lasting Value,* Jossey-Bass, 2004.

Gerstner, L., *Who Says Elephants Can't Dance?: Leading a
  Great Enterprise Through Dramatic Change,* HarperCollins, 2002.

Goleman, D., *Emotional Intelligence: Why It Can Matter
  More Than IQ,* Bantam, 1995.

Gray, J., *Men are from Mars, Women are from Venus,*
  Harper Collins, 1992.

Hamel, G. and Prahalad, C.K., *Competing for the Future,*
  Harvard Business School Press, 1994.

Hanh, T., *Living Buddha, Living Christ*, Riverhead Trade, 1997.

Hawkins, D., *Power Vs. Force: The Hidden Determinants of Human Behavior*, Hay House, 2002.

Jaworski, J., *Synchronicity*, Berrett-Koehler, 1996.

Kotter, J., *Leading Change*, Harvard Business School Press, 1996.

Kouzes, J. and Posner, B., *The Leadership Challenge*, Jossey-Bass, 2002.

Kremeer, Ruzzuto and Case, *Managing by the Numbers*, Perseus Publishing, 2000.

Krishnamurti, J., *Total Freedom: The Essential Krishnamurti*, Harper, 1996.

Leonard, G. and Murphy, M., *The Life We Are Given*, Penguin, 1995.

Levine, J., *The Enneagram Intelligences: Understanding Personality for Effective Teaching and Learning*, Bergin and Garvey, 1999.

Mandela, N., *Long Walk to Freedom*, Little Brown, 1994.

Maslow, A., *Maslow on Management*, Wiley, 1998.

Nisargadatta Maharaj, S., *I Am That*, The Acorn Press, 1973

Oakley, E. and Krug, D., *Enlightened Leadership*, Simon & Schuster, 1991.

Peters, T. and Waterman, R., *In Search of Excellence*, Harper & Row, 1982.

Spencer, L., *Winning Through Participation*, Kendall-Hunt, 2001.

Sogyal Rinpoche, *The Tibetan Book of the Living and the Dying*, HarperCollins, 1994.

Stansfield, B., *The Art of Focused Conversation*, ICA Canada, 1997.

Steil, L. and Bommelje, R., *Listening Leaders, Beaver's Pond Press*, 2004.

Talbot, M., *The Holographic Universe*, Harper Collins, 1991.

Tichy, N. and Devanna, M., *The Transformational Leader*, Wiley, 1990.

Tolle, E., *The Power of Now*. New World Library, 1999.

Woodsmall, M. and Woodsmall, W., *People Pattern Power: P3: The Nine Keys to Business Success*, Next Step Printers, 1999.

Zukav, G., *The Dancing Wu Li Masters – An Overview of the New Physics*, William Morrow & Co., 1979.

ABOUT THE AUTHOR

EDWARD MORLER, M.B.A., Ph.D.

Dr. Morler is CEO of Morler International, Inc., a management training and consulting firm specializing in interpersonal and organizational effectiveness. His specialties are negotiation skills training; executive coaching; and custom design and delivery of integrated programs dealing with integrity, leadership, developing emotional maturity, and organizational revitalization.

Dr. Morler's clients have included *Alcatel USA, Inc.; ARCO; AT&T; Banc One; Budapest Business Journal; Calgary Regional Health Authority; CGSAT Hungary Kft; Citicorp; City of Los Angeles; Colours International, Inc.; Euro-Phoenix Ltd.; Federal Reserve Bank of San Francisco, First National Bancorp; Firstar Corporation; Goldman, Sachs & Company; Harris Trust and Savings Bank; Hughes Aircraft; LG&E Energy, Lucent Technologies; Pacific Bell; Portola Systems; Regions Bank; Smith & Nephew; State Property Agency of Hungary; Toyota Motor Sales, Union Planters Bank, USA, Inc.; Union Bank of California; USAA; and Wells Fargo Bank.*

In addition to extensive work in the United States, Dr. Morler has conducted negotiations and/or training in *Canada, Mexico, Costa Rica, Ecuador, England, France, Germany, Hungary, Indonesia, Singapore, Thailand, Hong Kong, and the People's Republic of China.*

Additional Professional Experience

Prior to founding Morler International, Inc., in 1978, Dr. Morler was a management consultant for Fry Consultants, Inc.; Director of

Administrative Services, Air Line Pilots Association; Special Consultant to the Department of Labor; Executive Vice President of Sidney A. Fine Associates; and Senior Trainer for Effective Communication Skills, Inc. He served as a U.S. Naval Officer for four years in the Far East, Mediterranean, and Caribbean.

Education

Dr. Morler received his B.S. from Illinois Institute of Technology, his M.B.A. from the University of Chicago, his Ph.D. from the University of Maryland, and he is a graduate of the University of San Diego's Executive Management Program. He is also certified in Neuro-Linguistic Programming (NLP) and Thought Field Therapy (TFT).

Other

Dr. Morler is a frequent guest lecturer at conferences and management meetings. He has written in the areas of organizational and individual psychology, leadership, the dynamics of change, responsibility, and willingness. He is an Eagle Scout. He resides in Sonoma, California, with his wife, De, and their four Cockapoos.

Morler International, Inc. offers customized training programs integrating the development of emotional maturity with selected functional core competencies.

Programs include:

- Leadership and Management Development
- Negotiation Skills
- Customer and Interpersonal Relations
- Presentation Skills

Executive coaching is available to corporate clients.

For more information, please visit www.Morler.com.

To order copies of *The Leadership Integrity Challenge* please visit www.SanaiPublishing.com.

"The Leadership Integrity Challenge provides a unique approach for understanding the qualities and characteristics of the emotionally wise leader. In the current environment where corporations are struggling to regain trust, investors are looking for leadership that embodies integrity, strategic vision, and the ability to build a strong team. This is a 'must read' for the CEO who is building a team or assessing a current one. Dr. Morler clearly identifies the levels of emotional maturity as a basis for determining a team candidate or, in the case of an existing team, who stays and who goes."
    – Lou Thompson, Jr., CEO, National Investor Relations Institute

"The Leadership Integrity Challenge is an intelligent, very practical and resourceful guide on creating authentic leadership within yourself and others. It makes you think and provides the means to put concepts into action. Highly recommended."
    – Marjorie Winegrow, Director, SAGE Scholars Program,
        UC Berkeley; Chair., Business and Leadership Forum,
            Commonwealth Club of San Francisco

"Dr. Morler's impressive work struck me on a gut level, for here was the blueprint, clearly, of what I needed to do to more fully live my potential. Its poignant truth was both scary and exciting. I felt compelled to read on. I was not disappointed. This is a must read for those courageous souls who take the warrior's journey of fundamental change – be they heads of State, CEO's, or those on a path of personal growth."
    – Orlando Villanueva-Cortez, former Professor, Purdue University

"The *Leadership Integrity Challenge* teaches us how to respond and live a life of emotional maturity. This is required reading!"
    – Bill Keener, Regional Credit Director, Regions Bank

"In *The Leadership Integrity Challenge,* Ed Morler provides practical distinctions, clear insights, and an inspiring vision of integrity and leadership. His book challenges all leaders to work on themselves. This is not only a 'must read,' but a book that those committed to ongoing growth will refer to over and over again."
— Eleanor Bloxham, President, The Value Alliance and Corporate Governance Alliance and author of *Economic Value Management* and *Value-Led Organizations*

"This book is a gem! It is focused, relevant, insightful, actionable and filled with useful anecdotes and quotes. It flows and develops beautifully, has depth and makes sense from A to Z. It is indeed a 'how to' book of substance."
— Larry West, former E.V.P., Banc One

"Invaluable! An insightful presentation of the key elements that shape how we deal with life and relationships. It eloquently points out why integrity is about growing up — personally, professionally, and organizationally — and how we can go about it. It should be, at a minimum, a foundational text for any program dealing with personal growth or interpersonal skill development."
— Rod Pieper, Executive Coach

"Presence, impact, power, the list goes on and on. Dr. Morler presents a guide for not only monitoring and managing our own emotional maturity levels, but that of our associates, families, and friends as well. He encourages us to embrace our emotions and responsibly express them, allowing them to work for us rather than against. Dr. Morler has resounded a call for leaders — real leaders. Do you have what it takes?"
— Latoya Love, student, University of Wisconsin